G000243054

Solution Fo
Thinking in Schools

Behaviour, reading and organisation

John Rhodes and
Yasmin Ajmal

First published March 1995
Published by BT Press
17 Avenue Mansions, Finchley Road, London NW3 7AX

© John Rhodes and Jasmine Ajmal 1995

Layout by Alex Gollner

No part of this publication may be reproduced, stored in a retrieval
system, or transmitted in any form or by any means, electronic,
mechanical, photocopying, recording or otherwise, without the permission of the copyright owner.

ISBN 1 871697 69 7

Contents

ACKNOWLEDGMENTS

Many people have helped us with our thinking and ideas. We would like to thank the following: Tony Cline, Norah Frederikson, Evan George, Denny Grant, Roger Hancock, Chris Iveson and Jane Lethem.

We would also like to thank Alan Robertshaw for his technical assistance with the computer.

We would like to thank the Association of Educational Psychologists for allowing us to use sections from "The use of solution focused brief therapy in schools", Educational Psychology in Practice Vol 9, No 1 (pp 27-34).

CHAPTER ONE
The Solution Focused approach

Introduction

Within the field of family therapy a new and distinct approach has developed during the last few years, called Solution Focused Brief Therapy (de Shazer, 1985). Though it originated in family therapy practice it has evolved into an approach which can be used just as well with individuals as with families and other groups. On one level the solution focused approach has a set of very practical and sometimes simple procedures; on another level it contains ideas and theories which challenge many assumptions both in therapeutic thinking and in various areas of applied psychology. Furthermore, though these ideas and practices started in the context of 'therapy', we believe that this way of thinking can be transferred to other settings and ways of working: the work described in this book is more accurately thought of as consultation or casework of various kinds. Our emphasis is, therefore, very much on solution focused thinking for the everyday problems of school and not on therapy as such. In order, however, to understand this way of thinking we will need, in the first chapter, to explain in detail the work and ideas of solution focused therapists.

Various forms of family therapy have now been used and adapted in the school setting (Aponte, 1976; Dowling and Osborne, 1985). These writers developed the use of 'joint meetings', where family members and relevant school staff met together in the school setting to discuss concerns and develop therapeutic interventions. The use of solution focused therapy in schools is a very recent application. Kral (1987) has explained the use of solution focused methods with schools, and Molnar and Linquist (1989) give detailed accounts of a mixture of strategic and solution focused methods. Additionally, Durrant (1993) focuses on behaviour problems in schools. This book is intended to complement these publications, but also describes how the solution focused approach can be used in the context of developing reading programmes and with organisational work such as classroom management. All the work described took place in school and involved either direct work with students and their parents or indirect work with teachers. (We will use the terms 'student' and 'pupil' interchangeably). We have found the approach helpful for both school based and home based work with behavioural difficulties. Students may or may not have had difficulties in both places. This book, however, concentrates on interventions in schools.

In this introductory chapter we will outline the basic principles and techniques underlying solution focused brief therapy and the ways these can be used in interviews. Some of the techniques are specifically question driven, whilst other principles or assumptions operate as general route maps suggesting directions to explore or avoid. We have drawn particularly on the ideas of de Shazer (1985, 1988, 1991, 1994) and his various associates; these sources formed the bedrock of our work. The two most accessible introductions, we have found, are O'Hanlon and Weiner-Davies (1989) and George, Iveson and Ratner (1990). We have, however, also been strongly influenced by White and Epston (1990, 1992) whose approach, for convenience, could be termed 'narrative'; these writers would not categorise themselves as solution focused, but we have found their ideas to be related and compatible with this approach. Furman and Ahola (1992) likewise draw on both of these influences. This chapter is intended to provide a framework and a source of basic ideas for the later chapters in the book.

Some fundamental assumptions of Solution Focused therapy

O'Hanlon and Weiner-Davies (1987) discuss in detail many of the basic assumptions underlying solution focused brief therapy. These assumptions have not been proven experimentally but summarise the experience and observations of solution focused therapists.

1) An emphasis on the past and on details of the problem are not necessary for the development of solutions.

de Shazer (1985) argues that it is possible to do constructive work with clients by focusing on aspects which might provide ideas for solutions with, in some cases, very little discussion about the problem and its causation. There almost seems to be a logical break between problem talk and solution talk; the former does not automatically lead to the latter. Likewise, an extended discussion of the past will not necessarily lead to new ideas for solving problems in the present. Furthermore, for some clients extended discussion of the past can actually be unhelpful, for example, where it leads to feelings of hopelessness.

Most solution focused therapists are not saying, however, that it is never useful to discuss the past and details of problems. de Shazer (1994) mentions how it may be useful where a client has never put something into words before and Dolan (1992) suggests that it may be required where there are issues of trauma and abuse. However, solution focused therapists have found that in many cases it is more useful to spend the bulk of the time on the search for solutions. In the school context we have found this an invaluable insight and believe our experience confirms this observation.

2) There are always exceptions, that is, times when the problem is less or absent.

At the core of solution focused therapy is a network of ideas partly derived from observation of clinical work, and partly from theorising. It is claimed that where a problem is said to exist there are always exceptions, that is, times when the problem occurs less or not at all, and this is so even if the client isn't aware of these exceptions. For example, a person who is depressed may have days when they feel less depressed, or a child who usually rejects school may sit and work if given a page of sums to do.

These exceptions are often forgotten, ignored, or considered to be non-deliberate spontaneous 'flukes' (de Shazer, 1985, 1988). If, however, they are carefully explored, many ideas or clues can be found to suggest a possible solution. To give a simple example: if a discussion focuses on a child who is finding it difficult to develop relationships with other children, the interest will be on those times when a degree of positive interaction has been observed. This could be something as simple as sharpening pencils with another child. An exploration of what is different about this situation when the desired behaviour is occurring, may provide clues which can be used to help the child develop their social skills in other areas.

3) Clients have resources to resolve their difficulties.
Underlying all the above is the belief that people have within them the skills they will need to change and to solve their problems. People often emphasise their difficulties, their failures, times when they are ineffectual. Solution focused therapists seek to open up the possibilities of a different view, drawing attention to strengths and coping strategies. Even amidst the most distressing account of a person's life the question, "How did you cope?", can create the perspective of someone who has managed to survive and carry on.

One of the greatest influences in this area is Erickson (O'Hanlon, 1987). Erickson advocated using a client's own resources, strengths , beliefs and behaviour in the direction of change and called this "utilisation". de Shazer (1985) wrote, "this is the key to brief therapy; utilising what the client brings with him to meet his needs in such a way that the client can make a satisfactory life for himself".

4) A small change can lead to widespread changes.
Solution focused therapists argue that if one small positive improvement or change can be achieved in what was otherwise a repetitive stuck pattern, then many other positive changes can occur through the "ripple effect" (de Shazer, 1985). O'Hanlon and Weiner-Davies (1989) make the claim that change can arise from doing things differently, viewing what you are doing in a different way, or maybe both. Most importantly, the choice of the direction of this change lies with the client (within moral and legal parameters).

5) Clients have different ways of co-operating in therapy.
Another fundamental idea is the principle of co-operation. An intervention or question is not used if it is thought to disturb the co-operative relationship developing between therapist and client. de Shazer (1984) wrote:

"Each family (individual or couple) shows a unique way of attempting to co-operate, and the therapist's job becomes first, to describe that particular manner to himself..."

The principle of co-operation is a guide to action, and O'Hanlon (1987) suggests that if the activity of the therapist seems to be making the client uncomfortable, then the therapists should reconsider their course of action. For example, if the client seems to particularly wish to continue the discussion of his or her difficulties, then that might be the best course of action at that moment. The therapist, however, continues to listen for constructive possibilities which can be used at a later time (Lipchick, 1987).

Solution focused therapists also co-operate by noting and sometimes using the exact language, metaphors and ideas a person uses in describing their situation. There is, in fact, an effort to see the world from the client's point of view, to try to ascertain their belief-system. The client's language might well be used in discussing a task or in rephrasing questions. For example, a colleague described a woman who, in response to a question about what her preferred way of living might be, asked whether this meant what life would be like if it were "sweet". Using this term then aided communication.

There is also co-operation by focusing on what concerns the client, and not asking questions which imply other problems and weaknesses. If out of the blue, a therapist asks, "Has your child witnessed marital disputes?", the question might convey information such as, "I think they might have done", or that marital difficulties are the cause of the problem. Of course, most workers would not ask such an extreme question, yet many traditional diagnostic questions are not so dissimilar. The solution focused therapist tries to use language very carefully. O'Hanlon and Weiner-Davis (1989) advocate the use of questions which suggest the likelihood of change. For example, they prefer, "When the problem is solved, what hobbies might you choose?", as opposed to asking, "If the problem is solved ...?" In addition, solution focused therapists generally believe that questions give information to clients just as much as they obtain answers. Hence, questions can inadvertently encourage or discourage clients by the way they are constructed. This attention to language is found in all solution focused therapies and has become a major theme (de Shazer, 1991 and 1994, White and Epston, 1990).

6) The centrality of goals.

Solution focused therapists believe that if the client's goal is ignored or is not central, then the work together is unlikely to suceeed. Hence, in most cases, the therapist works in the direction the client wishes to take and does not impose aims taken from psychological theories about how people are supposed to live. If a goal seems unrealistic or too large, the aim will then be to negotiate which part of the goal is a feasable step foward. (Of course, the usual limitations apply such as not working with illegal or dangerous goals).

Where several people are involved, consideration of how the goals may be in conflict or vary becomes very important. The task may then be to clarify this situation before progress can be made.

Elements of Solution Focused interviewing

The following section shows how these assumptions are realised in practice.

Problem-free talk

Problem-free talk (George, Iveson, and Ratner, 1990) is a natural two-way conversation with a client that can focus on work, family and friends, interests, etc. The therapists may also say something about themselves in relation to the topic of conversation. It can be used at the beginning of a session to develop rapport between the client and the therapist; it can also be used to focus on areas of the person's life which are going well and which illustrate their competence. Some of these strengths and resources may be useful when looking at changes the client would like to make in other areas of their life. An interesting example was reported by Lethem (1994). A woman who some time ago had been in therapy, returned with her son because he had recently become involved in stealing. The son sat hunched up in his coat looking down at the ground. During the session the therapist asked about the woman's job and how she managed to co-ordinate life as a working mother. As the woman began explaining how she had taught her sons to cook (starting with a cup of tea and progressing to Sunday lunch), the son also joined in to expand on some of the details. A very warm picture of family life emerged with some clear examples of good parenting which provided a positive base from which the three of them could begin to look at the changes the family wished to make.

Not all therapists begin with a period of problem-free talk, while others may return to it later in the session or in later stages of the work (for example, if a different member of a family joins a session). In some situations the client wants to start talking immediately about the problem and this must be respected; however the session starts, the therapist will listen out for strengths and note them.

Exceptions

A general opening question to explore any possible exceptions might be:

> "Is there a time when (the complaint) does not occur, or occurs less than at other times?" (Lipchik and de Shazer, 1986).

However, it is often easier for a client to answer a more specific question such as:

> "When does your daughter listen to you?"
> "Have you ever noticed a time when Fred is able to play with other children without fighting?"
> "What's the closest things have come to you feeling calm when working with this child?"

Some therapists (O'Hanlon and Weiner-Davies, 1989) suggest using the most positive wording possible and would prefer a question such as, "Tell me about the times he does work?" as opposed to, "Are there times he does work?" We have found both useful: which one to use seems to be an issue of finding what best fits the particular context. In general we prefer the former, especially when a meeting seems to be in a more "positive mood".

If an exception is suggested, the therapist does not use a single question, but a sequence of questions (Lipchick, 1987). For example:
"What's different about those times?"
"What do you do differently?"
"Who else is involved, or notices these differences?"
"How could more of that happen?"
"How do you explain these differences?"
"How did you get that to happen?"

By encouraging a detailed examination of what is happening differently it may be possible to use some of the information to plan what to do next. It can also help a person to look again at a time when they had, in fact, been effective, thus opening up possibilities that they could be so again. The distinction between a deliberate and a spontaneous exception (de Shazer, 1988) is an important one (see Brewin, 1988, for a recent summary of attribution theory which covers a similar area). It will be easier for someone to repeat a behaviour they deliberately carried out than one they think "just happened". For example, when asking one mother what she was doing differently when her child did follow a request, she replied, "I was much firmer".

In trying to conceptualise which areas to explore for exceptions, particularly for aggressive behaviour, a range of contrasts can be considered. For example:
- good behaviour in contrast to outbursts of temper;
- partial outburst in contrast to total outbursts;
- times when it might have occurred, but didn't, in contrast to times when it did.

Hence, an exception might be when a desirable but rare behaviour did occur or when an undesirable behaviour didn't occur, or occurred with less intensity, or was amenable to discussion, and so on. For aggressive behaviour such as fighting, it is also interesting to note those times when a confrontation almost occurred but didn't accelerate; did other people do something different or did the student find alternative means of resolving the situation? If it was the latter, then the student can be recognised as sometimes acting in responsible and caring ways.

The search for exceptions can be in the present or past. Kral (1987) suggests asking teachers if they have had similar problems in the past, and how they solved them at that time. This may help the teacher to remember forgotten strengths or strategies which can then be reworked to accommodate the new situation. Another rich source of information can be provided by looking at the improvements which may have occurred in the time between the referral and the first session. Weiner-Davies, de Shazer, and Gingerich (1987) call this "pre-session change". A question can be asked to encourage the noticing of these when arranging an interview:

"Between now and the time we meet note down any differences which occur."

This is deliberately vague to encourage the person to focus on the things which are meaningful to them. In the session it can then be followed up by questions such as :

"How come you did this?"

"How did you reach that decision?"

"What is it about your children that made you feel they could take on this responsibility?"

With some clients, the bulk of the first session can revolve around exceptions. Sometimes it is difficult for people to recall any exceptions and a common initial response is, "I don't know". However, this could just mean that the client has not thought about their situation in this way before and it is worth the therapist persisting in the belief that there are times when things are closer to how the client would like them to be. Furthermore, an exception might well appear at some later stage when talking about an area of the person's life which is at some distance from the original problem. For example, a parent concerned about their child's difficult behaviour might comment that he is well-liked by someone. Exploring what is happening in this "exception" may offer some clues relevant to the original problem.

Goals

The negotiation of goals can take place at any time during a session and can be returned to or modified during and between sessions. The clearer, more specific and more realistic these goals are, the more likely it is that the client will attain them. Some clients can readily identify their objectives, others are often more preoccupied with ending something or escaping a situation and they need assistance to build a picture of what they would like to happen instead. Alternatively, a person may have a vague notion of what they want, for example, "I want to be happy", and need to develop a clearer picture of what that would look like; that is, what they will be doing when they are happy, how they will know when they are happy, what will be the first signs that they are feeling happier? If someone remains vague in spite of the above sorts of questions, then de Shazer (1994) suggests using scaling questions (see later section). Sometimes people are clear about what their goal is but it seems such a huge step they can easily feel overwhelmed and give up. When talking with children about reading they often have no idea of the progress they may have made, and have not thought about what the next step might be. However, discussions focusing on what they already know and what would be a sign they were improving can help to break the task into smaller units where success can be envisaged.

An immediate goal for a session can be identified by the very first question:

"What would you like to achieve from this session? What would you like to talk about that would make you feel that coming here had been worthwhile?"

To identify longer-term goals a question can be asked such as:
"How will you know the problem is finally over?"

This again helps the person define what it is they are looking for. It is often also helpful to explore the views of significant others (the person's

partner, parents, friends etc.) in the attempt to construct precise and concrete goals. For example:
> "Who would be the first to notice you had moved toward your goal?"
> "What might they notice?"
> "How will (your boyfriend) know when the jealousy problem is solved?" (de Shazer, 1988).

Hypothetical solutions
A further claim of solution focused brief therapy is that sometimes clients have no vision of "life without the problem" (de Shazer, 1988; Furman and Ahola, 1992). They find it difficult to think of a time when the problem did not exist or to envisage a time when it could ever be solved. In some cases people lose hope that their situation will ever change. If, on the other hand, they are asked to describe life without the problem in as much detail as possible, then sometimes clues and suggestions emerge that suggest what a person could do now to change his or her predicament, and also emphasise where a person wants to get to, that is, what their goals might be. For this purpose, de Shazer (1988) designed the 'miracle question':
> "Suppose that one night, while you were asleep, there was a miracle and this problem was solved. The miracle occurs while you are sleeping so you do not immediately know that it has happened. When you wake up, what is the first thing you will notice that will let you know that there has been a miracle?"
> "What would be the first signs that the miracle had happened?"
> "What would you find yourself doing that will be a sign of the miracle?"
> "Who else would notice that the miracle had happened? How would you know they had noticed?"

The picture which emerges is elaborated in as much detail as possible by encouraging the client to describe the situation as they would like it to be. This can help them to focus on something they are already doing, or something they might like to try.

One assumption behind the miracle question is that some of the activities described by the client, even seemingly quite incidental ones, may be very useful activities for inducing the desired goal. For example, one woman experiencing panic attacks talked about how she would get herself a new wardrobe of clothes in her "miracle" world (de Shazer, 1988). This could then be explored in further detail, for example, by asking how she could plan to do this, where she would go, would she ask someone to go with her, what sort of clothes would she buy, what would be the signs to her that she was ready to undertake a trip of this nature? Thus, what could have simply been construed as a passing thought was translated into activities which could help to bring about significant change.

Sometimes people locate their miracle in something external to themselves, for example, an additional teacher or a special school. It is often not helpful to get immediately locked in a discussion about whether this is possible, but rather to explore this "miracle" with questions such as:

"Ideally, what would meet this student's needs? How would things be arranged? What would be provided?"

"How will you know this resource has been useful?"

"What differences would you notice?"

"How would you use the resources?"

"What will you be doing differently?"

"What changes would someone else notice?"

A further strategy we have found useful in helping a client focus on the future is to ask them to imagine that a month has passed and the situation is as they would like it be. This is followed by a series of questions asking the client to describe what is happening and the steps they will have taken to enable the things they have described to happen.

Rating scales

The first steps towards achieving goals can be explored through rating scales where 1 equals the worst things have ever been and 10 equals the best things could be. The client can be asked where they would place themselves on the scale, what they have done or can do to put themselves at that point, and how they would know they had reached the next point on the scale. We have also found it useful to ascertain what would be an acceptable point to reach on the scale - not everyone wants to get to 10 and may be quite satisfied with a 6.

On one occasion, a teacher stated that a student's behaviour had improved. She was then asked:

"If 1 was equivalent to Conrad's behaviour at its worst, and 10 near perfect, where is he now?"

She stated that recently his behaviour had been about 5, but had previously been at 3, when we first spoke. To this type of response questions can be asked such as:

"What has happened to move Conrad's behaviour from a 3 to a 5?"

"How confident are you that his behaviour will keep at a 5?"

"What would increase your confidence?"

Answers to such questions can sometimes give detailed information. One mother in reply to a scaling question said that evidence of her child moving up the scale would be that he would spontaneously accept the offer of going swimming with a woman from next door.

The particular and, we believe, creative emphasis of the solution focused approach is to work with the client to construct a picture of how he or she will know that the first steps are being made towards both short and long-term goals and, hence, how they can measure progress (de Shazer, 1988). The issue of "knowing" and describing the goal vividly cannot be overstated; we have found this to be one of the most useful techniques. O'Hanlon and Weiner Davies (1989) emphasise this by the use of a 'video description'. For example, "If you have solved the problem and a video was made of you in your problem-free life what exactly would I see you do?" One question that can be very useful in beginning this description is: "What will the first signs of progress be?"

Besides goal identification, scaling questions can also be used to ascertain a person's confidence in a change and their motivation to try something out. The use of confidence rating scales can also be enormously valuable in high-lighting some of the barriers to progress which can then be addressed. For example :

> ‘ "On a scale of 1-10 where 1 denotes no confidence and 10 equals full confidence, how confident are you that you will be able to carry out this task?"
>
> "What would help you feel more confident you could move to the next point on the scale?"

A girl was asked this in relation to reading regularly at home. She placed herself at 2. However, she thought she would feel a little more confident if she were able to read to someone. The lady who lived upstairs was identified as someone the girl liked reading to and this was subsequently set up.

Tasks and compliments

Towards the end of the session the therapist may take a short break out of the room to re-read notes, reflect on the information that has been discussed and think about how to round off the session. Although this seems very strange at first it can be invaluable in collecting thoughts before feeding them back. After the break, the solution focused therapist usually begins with one or several compliments. These are observations of exceptions, strengths, resources, motivation and so on. We believe that these should be genuine observations delivered in a deliberate, calm and friendly way. To a teacher, a compliment could be: "I think you've worked really hard to help Joseph settle in class, and it's certainly been a difficult job." Once the habit of looking for strengths in the lives of clients is begun, it is surprising how many can be found.

Compliments can be followed by some general discussion of relevant ideas and issues and a task may be suggested. There are two basic kinds of tasks, "observation" tasks and "doing" tasks. The type of task will depend to some extent on the attitude of the client towards change and towards the therapist. For some clients the context they find themselves in is not relevant to their interests, or they might have been obliged to attend the session: de Shazer (1985) suggests that this could be described as having a visitor relationship to the therapist. Another group are concerned and willing to give a lot of information, but do not believe their actions could have any effect; this group have been called "complainants" (we prefer the term "information givers"). A third group who believe their actions could bring about change, are called "customers" (de Shazer, 1985). These three categories tend to define "positions" towards the therapist, since the same client could have a different relationship to another therapist, or could, in fact, change their attitude within the session. We have found these distinctions very useful in the school context since it is not a rare occurrence for someone, particularly students but also parents and teachers, to be "sent to see" the psychologist, hence making it very difficult to decide "who, exactly, is the client." Directly addressing this reluctance, and ending an interview if the client so wishes, greatly assists communication and future co-operation. In such situations the most motivated customer is, perhaps, the referrer and not the person in the room; hence, it would be better to work with the former and not the latter.

The therapist co-operates by only giving tasks and ideas which "fit" the client's construed expectations and yet at the same time suggest new information or new possibilities. If a client seems highly motivated, then a doing task is indicated. For example if exception questions have revealed several examples of "what works", then the tasks might simply be to do more of this. Sometimes the task just slightly modifies the exception behaviour, or a list could be made of exception behaviours and a suggestion made that the client try one per day.

If a client seems less motivated, or only sees their role as information giver, then an observation task can be suggested. An example might be:
"Notice times when Kelly does seem to be making the first steps towards making friends with other pupils."

In general, customers will do tasks, information-givers will tend to do observation tasks, and visitors will do neither. If a task has been given and not carried out, then this feedback suggests that further tasks of this nature are inappropriate (de Shazer, 1985). In the solution focused approach the therapist does not argue or show disappointment with a client for modifying or not doing a task. Rather, this is seen as essential feedback on the client's situation and as a guide to whether tasks should be given and if so, what kind. There is no "test" for a client's position, but an impression arises from comments made and the response to tasks.

Teachers are often in the position of being "information-givers" since they are concerned, yet feel overwhelmed by their workload and believe the cause of the problem lies outside the classroom. Hence, complicated and time-consuming interventions are not likely to be carried out, even if polite agreement was given.

An interesting innovation of de Shazer was the development of "formula tasks" (de Shazer, 1985). These can be used for many different kinds of problems and situations. One such task is:

"Between now and the next time we meet, we (I) would like you to observe, so that you can describe to us (me) next time, what happens in your (pick one: family, life, marriage, relationship) that you want to continue have happen." (de Shazer, 1985).

Another very useful task is:

"Notice what you do, when you overcome the urge to ...", for example, the urge to shout (de Shazer 1985).

Some formula tasks do involve actions, though they may not be specified. One is the "Do something different" task (de Shazer, 1985), where the client is asked to do something different, however strange, in a situation where they have previously repeated a set response which isn't working for them. For example, de Shazer (1985) describes a case where a young woman was worried that in spite of all efforts her husband often came home depressed and usually became worse: she was given the "do something different" task and carried out a whole series of new actions such as being out of the house. The change in interaction patterns had a positive effect.

The trend in the writings of de Shazer is toward ever greater simplicity. In his recent book (1994), the tasks used tend to concern doing more of what works and observation of movement toward goals. In our work we have also found that some of the simplest questions and tasks were the most useful and that we did not need to use complicated tasks. Furthermore, if in doubt about what to do, we tended to just use compliments.

The general pattern of first and subsequent sessions

Great efforts have been made by de Shazer (1988) and his team to "map" the decisions and directions made in a first session and subsequent ones. The following is a simple guide drawing on suggestions made by O'Hanlon and Weiner-Davies (1989).

In the first session questions tend to proceed as follows:

a) look for strengths or exceptions of any kind to the presenting concern; quite often the whole session can be spent doing this. In addition, throughout the session the therapist will return to the topic of clarifying with the client tangible goals they can work towards.

b) Next, many therapists use hypothetical solution questions, especially if (a) did not produce many exceptions or clear goals.

c) If both (a) and (b) are insufficient, return to a consideration of the problem and any suggested goals. For example, have they been misunderstood? In this situation an observation task is the only one likely to be given.

In the second, and all subsequent sessions, the therapist tends to do the following:

a) if something has worked well, or a little bit, suggest doing more, and explore in as much detail as possible aspects of these changes. This discussion can often centre around scaling questions. For example:

"What was your rating on the scale in the last session?"

"Where would you place yourself today?"

The answers to these questions can form the prelude to exploring differences. If there have been improvements these can be explored through a series of questions such as:

"What is different?"

"What have you done differently to achieve these changes?"

"Who will have noticed the changes? What will they have noticed?"

"What does this tell you about yourself?"

"How confident are you that you will be able to maintain these changes?"

"What would increase your confidence?"

"Where would you like to get to?"

If the second session starts with the client giving only negative information, O'Hanlon and Weiner-Davis suggest that the therapists should persevere with gentle exception questions or detailed questions about change to make sure the latter have not occurred. Quite often a session can begin with the client reporting the worse things that have occurred, and only begin to mention positive changes if asked.

No methods work for all clients. If no progress is reported, O'Hanlon and Weiner-Davis state that they would ask themselves a series of questions such as, "Who is the customer?" and, "What is the problem?". The aim of such questions is to consider whether the therapist has developed 'fit' with the client. Solution focused therapists tend to keep trying out different ideas and in some situations draw upon skills they might have learnt from other models of therapy, though given a solution focused emphasis. For example, O'Hanlon tends to use hypnotherapy to look for "unconscious solutions" and we will later give an example of using a contract.

The outline for the sessions given above is, of course, only approximate. Actual sessions are more complex; certain areas may need returning to several times. Working in the context of the school also necessitates great flexibility since all the participants are rarely available at the same time and situations tend to change rapidly (for instance, where a pupil is near to being excluded).

Practical arrangements

Solution focused therapists will work with individuals, families, or groups, in fact, with whoever attends a session. The rationale behind this is that the whole family or "system" need not be present in the room for change to occur. Individual members, especially if motivated, can be very powerful in instigating new actions.

Sessions tend to last an hour, with a five to ten minute break before the final message or ideas are discussed with the clients. In school work we vary this considerably, but do find having a break to re-read our notes and to think of ideas an invaluable practice. This type of work can be done solo or with a team. The average number of sessions for de Shazer and his team is approximately 4.6 (de Shazer, 1991); however, it is not unusual to have as few as one or two sessions.

Other influences on our work

Most of the work outlined in this book uses the structure and techniques discussed in the above sections. However we have also been interested in ideas expressed by other therapists in this field. The following elements have been borrowed mainly, but not exclusively, from White and Epston (1990, 1992).

a) Externalisation.

This involves describing a problem as though it were something external to the person and often involves giving "it" a name. For example, a case is cited later (Christopher in chapter two) in which a child described his temper as a "ghost"; questions could then be asked such as "Do you know how to chase away this ghost?" This form of questioning emphasises a person's agency and in so doing introduces the idea that they can have some effect on the problem. With the problem described as an external entity, sometimes a humourous one, ways can then be discussed of coping with or changing its influence. This can also help to counteract the tendency of the individual or others to see the person as the problem.

Another example is of a six year old boy, William, who called the urge to steal, his "Bugs Bunny fingers". We then talked about ways he could thwart Bugs Bunny. The use of this name provided a meaningful way in which William could talk about his behaviour and remained the focus of discussion over several sessions.

The above examples are very colourful but the approach can also be very subtle. For example, if it emerges that a person holds a negative view of him or herself, then White might ask how the person was 'recruited' to this point of view and thereby emphasising a separation between person and problem.

b) Relative influence questioning.
Relative influence questioning (White, 1989) has two contrasting phases. After establishing the nature of the "problem", say, losing your temper, participants are first asked to describe the influence of the problem on any aspect of the family's life (actions, thoughts, descriptions of self and others, etc.). For example, losing your temper might mean there are lots of arguments; people don't like to eat together any more; the family rarely go out on trips. The second phase consists of asking how the family might affect and have an influence, in any way, on the "life" of the problem. White and Epson suggest that this form of questioning also encourages externalisation.

Since this process requires an initial focus on problem talk, we have tended not to use it to begin work with clients, but reserved it as an alternative approach if little or no progress is being made. A later casework example (Darren in chapter two) will illustrate this more fully.

c) Letter writing.
Besides the activities within a session, communication can occur between meetings. For example, we have experimented with writing letters to the client - a technique described by White and Epston (1990). These can be used in several ways: to summarise some of the main points raised during the discussion; to emphasise certain key points; to note down any subsequent thoughts which it may be helpful for the client to think about before the next session; to celebrate changes. These "afterthoughts" are often expressed as a question. The following is a hypothetical example based on an interview with a woman who was interested in developing her confidence in asserting her views.

"I was very interested to hear about the way you went up to Nina's school and talked to her teacher about needing to remember to give her some orange juice at break time (Nina was diabetic). You showed great understanding of the teacher's position but still managed to assert your views. You felt you were able to do this because it was for the good of Nina, even though you were very nervous. I wondered if there were any times you had managed to assert your views when it was to do with your own needs, and if you used the same approach or found something different?"

Other examples of letters are given in the following chapters. On some occasions the person has also written a letter to us in response to a specific request. For example, Darren was asked to design and send some charts on which he had recorded his behaviour in lessons. Having this "focus" can help provide a support for a student as a way of encouraging them to carry out a new course of action. This can be particularly useful when the school needs to see some evidence that a student is making an effort to change their behaviour.

d) The story of the self.
This is not a technique but rather a general conception. White and Epston (1992) suggest that over time individuals develop 'stories' about who and what they are. For example, "I am not the sort of person who ..." These stories, however, not only record the past but can also determine how people experience the world, and, as it were, suggest to them how to live their lives. Children who have a story about themselves which involves not being clever, may approach learning tasks, especially ones they are not familiar with, in the belief that they will not be able to do them. And they will remember previous times when they have found something difficult, thus confirming their view. However, there will also be plenty of evidence which suggests that they can in fact learn - for instance, learning how to talk. Sometimes these "stories" are overtly expressed, at other times they may be revealed by a throwaway comment. White and Epston suggest that by discussing with a person details and aspects which do not fit the "problem saturated" story the person may begin to see other possibilities, and may choose to develop a different self story, thus leading to new actions.

e) The use of metaphors.

We have found using metaphors (O'Hanlon, 1987) to aid communication very helpful when working with students experiencing difficulties in their learning and in general with students. For example, using hobbies as a basis for discussion we explore how they have learnt skills. One boy who had experienced a marked difficulty in developing his spelling was very interested in magic. He described how he learnt a new trick by splitting it up into small chunks, learning each chunk separately, putting the bits together and practising until he felt he could it without thinking about it. What a perfect way to learn new spellings!

This approach is explored in more detail in chapters three and four, which also contain some examples showing how it is used.

f) Reframing and normalisation: New descriptions.

Reframing and normalisation (a variation of reframing) refer to two techniques often used by solution focused therapists (Berg, 1991; O'Hanlon and Weiner-Davis, 1989), which in general derive from strategic family therapy (Watzlawick et al, 1974; Weakland, et al, 1974). A central idea for these therapists was that problems were associated with "stuck" interaction patterns. For example, where a couple repeatedly argue without resolving an issue. The reframe was developed to allow such a couple to see each other's actions in a different light. In a reframe the same "elements" or "facts" are given a new interpretation or description. In one case a boy's crying was seen as a possible sign of intelligence and sensitivity, as opposed to disturbance or awkwardness. The suggestion of different motives can be very useful in changing a stuck pattern of interacting and enables people to explore different ways of relating to each other. An example arose in a discussion about a boy who refused to read out loud in class and would often end up in confrontation with his teachers. After talking with the boy, his "defiance" was reframed as "embarrassment" that he might not know a word and that his classmates would make fun of him. This led to a discussion about how to increase his confidence in public situations - especially as he was, in fact, a very capable boy.

In normalisation, an action or thought is described as more or less "normal" in the circumstances; for example, it might be suggested that being argumentative, when under stress, is not unusual. It would seem that solution focused workers generally use these in a very low-key way, and do not attempt some of the complicated and unusual reframes of strategic therapy. The central function they can perform seems to be one of "new viewing" (O'Hanlon and Weiner-Davis, 1989), for instance, of realising that one's reaction to a situation was neither odd nor the sign of some yet deeper problem.

Concluding comment

Though the majority of the ideas described in this chapter were developed in the context of therapy, we have found that they can be extremely useful in the applied setting of the school, and also in non-therapy areas such as reading programmes and classroom management. In the following chapters we set out to illustrate how solution focused thinking can be used in such diverse contexts.

CHAPTER TWO

From conflict to co-operation

Introduction

The casework described in this chapter involves direct work with parents, the student and members of staff. Work of a strictly consultative nature, involving only discussions with teachers, is described in chapter five. The referrals were made by teachers, usually the head teacher, and typically, the following reasons or descriptions were given for referring a student:

- extreme aggression and anger
- fighting
- ignoring or insulting staff
- dangerous behaviour

Often the situation was thought to be moving towards a point where a student could no longer remain in the school, and might be facing a possible 'exclusion' if the difficult behaviour continued or accelerated.

None of our work involves special apparatus such as one-way mirrors, and is done in whatever room (hopefully comfortable) is available. Most of our work has been done solo; however, for just under two years we chose to work together one morning per week. We found this useful for dealing with difficult cases and as a means of developing our skills.

For any particular case, one of us would take the lead role, keeping responsibility for the case and making the final decisions, whilst the other member acted as an observer. On the next case, usually the same morning, we would swap roles. We did not, however, want the role of the observing member to be limited to silence as we thought this might be inhibiting for participants, and anyway, the observer would also sometimes want to join in. We therefore developed a "baton passing system", with the following guidelines:

1) The lead speaker makes the final decision on what directions and areas to explore while in the sessions.

2) If the observer wishes to ask a particular question within a specific theme or line of thought, for example, on exceptions, the observer may ask: "Do you mind if I ask a question in this area?"

3) If the observer thinks it might be useful to start a new line of exploration, he or she may ask: "If you've finished in this area, then it might be interesting to ask a hypothetical question?"

Before most sessions we had agreed on what areas would be explored, and any changes in direction or improvisation were agreed between us while in the room. If we became "stuck", then quite often we took an extra mini-break outside the room to discuss what to do.

We found this baton-passing system very useful. By working out an agreed and co-ordinated routine we were able to maintain our focus on creative sequences of themes and questions.

In the first part of this chapter we present a selection of our individual and team work in schools. The cases chosen are, of course, ones we regard as successes. However, we wish to assure the reader that this is not always the case. Learning to apply solution focused ideas could be compared to learning to play a game such as darts - the rules and principles are easy to learn, yet getting consistent bullseyes is very difficult. In the last part of the chapter we will draw out some general issues.

Case illustrations

The case illustration of **Christopher** represents a straightforward example of building on exceptions (as also does the case of Jim in chapter five), whereas the case of **Joe** shows how the solution focused approach plus the use of a contract was needed to pass through a very difficult phase. **Katrina** is an example of negotiating goals as the main focus of the work, in particular, helping someone choose a future path. **Leon** shows how we sometimes moved from a basic solution focused approach, based on the ideas of de Shazer, to the use of relative influence questions as a second phase, and one that widened the areas of inquiry; we regard this as an example of psychologists 'doing something different' when not making progress. The case of **Darren** shows how the story of self can be important and how someone can be held under the sway of a damaging explanation.

We have carried out our work with what we regard as a solution focused approach, using what seemed appropriate in the particular situation: it is, however, our interpretation and no doubt the same cases would be done in other ways by the original writers and others.

In some of the following write-ups, the work has been carried out by both authors, whilst other work was done individually.

Christopher (and the ghost)

The school first raised Christopher (aged 5 years 9 months) for discussion because of concerns about his outbursts of temper and throwing of things at students and staff. This was occurring every week. I was also informed that his parents had broken up the year before and that the problems had started around the same time. My notes record: "staff have asked Christopher why he has exploded. He says he doesn't know". In addition, the referral form stated that Christopher was likeable and could get along with most people, yet, "when his temper flares he is impossible and becomes extremely violent … When he is angry he seems to have no control."

A meeting was called: both parents, the class teacher and myself attended. Christopher was not at this meeting. In the first part of the meeting considerable time was dedicated to discussing Christopher's various strengths, how he was friendly, well-liked, good at reading and number work. Both the parents and the staff had clear goals that Christopher should stay in the school if possible, and that his good and creative behaviour, as opposed to his temper, should be displayed.

This discussion had contrasted his good behaviour as a major exception to the temper outbursts. In some cases building on the above sort of exceptions might well have been sufficient, but to find out would have taken considerable time. I thought it important for the group to try new arrangements as soon as possible since the problem behaviour was dangerous. The exceptions also seemed frequent and spontaneous, and it was thus difficult to see how they could be developed. The aim of the next series of questions, therefore, was to see if there were ever times when the various adults thought that an outburst might happen, but for whatever reason, had not done so; these would be exceptions to the acceleration of the problem pattern. Each adult present was asked, "How can we avoid his outbursts of temper?" A useful aspect of this question is that it places the behaviour in an interactional context of what others notice and do. Furthermore, the question does not ask for ideas about the cause of the problem (the danger being that any cause may be said to exist in the personality of the child). Each participant was given time to fully explain their point of view. His father said he could predict when Christopher was going to be difficult; he had "hyper days" when he "pushes ... pushes". If an adult then went in "heavy-handed", especially in public, there could be difficulties. He suggested that adults had to be firm yet very calm with him, they had to go "softly, softly". His mother had noted that if "rushed" in the mornings, Christopher started arguing, but also observed, "If I take time, he doesn't lose his temper." The teacher described how she could see a pattern of Christopher getting distracted, not concentrating, and then interfering with others.

At this point it seemed appropriate to summarise ideas and to refocus specifically on what could be done to help matters; the group was again asked for suggestions and these were written down. They included giving Christopher the job of being a tutor for the computer, making sure he had work which challenged him, providing extra mathematics, and giving him a lot of attention while at the same time going "softly, softly". At the end we discussed what to do if he did lose his temper; the school said he did calm down with the head teacher and hence they could cope with that for the moment. By the end of the meeting I had therefore collected exceptions about the times he was very well-behaved in class and about times when he didn't lose his temper. No direct suggestions were made by me to the parents as to what they might do, though our discussion had yielded several ideas. For the teacher I sent a list of the various ideas discussed, but emphasised that they should be used as the teacher saw fit.

Two weeks later another meeting took place; this time I spoke with the teacher and mother, and then briefly with Christopher and his mother together. Since the father could not come, I summarised the meeting in a letter:

Dear Ms Smith and Mr Jones,
I thought I would sum up the meeting held at Graystock Infants on the 18th of October.
The head and class teacher reported that during the 2 week period there had been no outbursts of temper from Christopher. Furthermore, Christopher had done some excellent work.
I was particularly impressed to hear that on the 17th, Christopher at one point said to his teacher that he was feeling angry. The teacher then found some quiet work for Christopher, and any trouble was avoided.
When I met Christopher I asked him how he had managed to control his temper. He said he knew but didn't tell us. I then asked him how he saw his temper. After some thought Christopher said his temper was like a "ghost". We wondered if at last Christopher was controlling this ghost and not the ghost telling Christopher what to do.
At the end we suggested meeting again in a few weeks, especially to see how Christopher is working.

Yours sincerely

John Rhodes
Educational Psychologist

The question asking how he "saw his temper" was an example of externalisation (White and Epston 1990). I am not sure it was really necessary in this case, but it did provide all three of us, including Christopher, with some amusement: this felt like a good way to finish our work together.
   I continued to discuss Christopher's progress each term with the head teacher; the crises subsided, though he did occasionally hit others. One and a half years later I was involved again; this time he had

been fighting in the playground. One meeting, celebrating his progress, building on strengths, and setting up a home reporting system, proved sufficient and the school said he stopped being of concern.

Joe

On the initial referral form Joe (age ten and a half years) was described as below average in reading and writing; the main concern, however, was his behaviour. In particular, this was written about him: "has displayed aggressive, uncontrolled behaviour towards other children and verbal abuse to adults in the school."

This proved to be a most difficult case, involving eight meetings. Towards the end I began to think that there could be no success, that Joe would have to leave the school and perhaps go to a special school. To illustrate the work, I shall describe part of the second session, and some techniques used at a later stage. The first few meetings I experienced as a kind of "see-saw" between terrible descriptions of Joe's violence and temper, and occasional exceptions. The first meeting had been with Joe and his mother; I asked about exceptions and used the miracle question. The end task had been to observe the good things they wished to continue in their family life.

The second session began with a flood of worrying information. In addition to Joe's fighting, his father had heart trouble and was waiting for an operation, and Joe himself was undergoing an examination of his hearing. During this first half it seemed necessary to listen to and record these negative problem focused accounts. Everyone at the meeting seemed upset and gave very long and detailed negative answers to any question, including solution focused ones. An exclusive focus on exceptions at this early stage could have proved counter-productive as there seemed to be a great need to explore the current situation and for an appreciation of the pressures on the family and school. de Shazer (1988) suggests, "When necessary, extract step-by-step descriptions of the complaint" (the guidelines, chapter six); fortunately, this tends to be rare, but this, I believed, was one. My questions, therefore, tended to be about coping and after some time I asked about "triggers" for his behaviour;

the teacher immediately said, "When Joe gets frustrated with his work or when jokes and play fighting get out of hand."

At this point the Head casually stated that Joe was "sensitive". From this one statement several other comments followed which implied a positive side to Joe's personality which had been dormant until now. For example, Joe was not spiteful, he was popular and was capable of having a serious conversation. This would prove to be an important theme returned to again and again. However, these likeable qualities were sometimes hidden because Joe saw himself as an outcast and often "put up a front".

After the break I listed all the stresses Joe seemed to be experiencing, such as his father's illness, his hearing problems and the prospect of transferring to secondary school in the near future when he was not making progress at this school. The aim of this was not to prove any causal connection, but just to wonder if there were any connections. In a sense I was "normalising" his behaviour, suggesting that his behaviour was not perhaps unreasonable given the circumstances. There is also a suggestion of strength since the individual is having to withstand all these pressures. This met with general agreement. I also focused on the "two sides" of Joe (an expression used by the head), that is, his "friendly, sensitive side" and his "temper". By these reflections I hoped to suggest an alternative to the very pathological viewpoints developing about Joe. I also wanted to suggest that having these two very different sides was puzzling.

A subsequent discussion with Joe directly focused on how he could avoid getting into a temper. In the work of Epston and White there is sometimes an emphasis on "how" a person may attempt to deal with a difficulty, particularly "temper tantrums" (for an example see chapter three of Epston and White, 1992). Joe could remember one instance when he had done this and subsequent questions focused on how he had managed it.

After some levelling off of his behaviour, a number of very serious incidents occurred leading to a three-day exclusion. To weather this storm I suggested a simple "contract" approach and a report book to take home. The contract entailed four steps which the school agreed to

follow should any difficulties occur. If, for example a warning had been given, but Joe continued to be rude to someone, then the teacher would move automatically to the next step. The four steps were:
- a final warning that his behaviour was unacceptable;
- a message to a helper;
- sending to another class;
- his parents to be contacted if he refuses.

This is an example of how solution focused work can be combined with other methods. In essence, the contract says: if you do X, Y will happen. Contracts need to be employed with caution, yet they have been found to be particularly useful in near emergency situations, where violence or a complete breakdown in a school placement seems imminent. A contract can circumvent this sudden and dramatic giving up. Within the context of a firm structure holding the situation, it then becomes easier to refocus on forgotten strengths and exceptions. Various contracts have been used by behaviourists (Tharp and Wetzel, 1969). The approach used here is somewhat different in that no specific recording of behaviour is required, nor are behaviour dependent rewards used. In this respect it is similar to that of Glasser (see Wolfgang and Glickman, 1986). The strength of contracts may lie in two sources: the student gets clear feedback on their actions and the school is required to act in clear and predictable ways.

At the next meeting things were still very difficult, the contract only just holding; to strengthen the latter required further solution focused questions. I focused on how the school could make this work better, that is, emphasising the parts that were working well and modifying those that were not in this particular situation.

On the way to the next meeting I was full of foreboding. To my astonishment there had been dramatic improvements. There had been no major incidents, Joe was more co-operative and had "worked his socks off". Joe himself appeared more cheerful and had been "as good as gold" at his grandmother's house. I asked everyone how they explained this excellent change. I wanted to help people to look in detail at the important elements which could then be repeated. It could also help to reinforce the strengths and skills of the people involved. A number of reasons were given. Joe's mother commented on his new hearing aid. The head teacher felt that the situation had been very "tight" for Joe after the exclusion. Joe's class teacher had noticed that Joe had not liked the time he had spent away from school and would have much preferred to have been there.

I believe an essential feature of this casework was the combination of two elements: on the one hand, a consistent emphasis on rare exceptions to the problem flooded accounts of difficult behaviour, but on the other, flexibility in the use of strategies. In particular, the use of contracts when the teacher seemed on the point of rejecting Joe might have given recognition that I and the head teacher knew how difficult things had become and thus gave some encouragement to the teacher. As is often said, solution focused work is not a naive simple emphasis on "positives": to ignore the momentary pessimism of the staff would have endangered co-operation. This case also illustrates how a young person can be under frightening pressures, yet not have them fully recognised. I wonder what would have happened if Joe had been "diagnose", for example, with some strange label such as "temper disordered"?

Darren

Darren, aged 12, was half way through his first year at an all-boys secondary school when we met him with his mother and the head of his year group. We were told he had made an excellent start during the first six weeks and that academically he was a rewarding student to work with. Since this time, however, his behaviour had deteriorated; he was constantly in trouble for fighting with other pupils and refusing to obey requests from teachers.

Although some improvements had been noted in the two weeks before the meeting the situation was getting more serious and there were feelings among some of the staff that Darren would not last the course. This latter sentiment was reflected in the head of year's rating of 5 on a scaling question (1 = not committed, 10 = very committed) exploring the school's commitment to Darren remaining there. However, the head of year was still willing to work with Darren, thus providing an important link between Darren's efforts and the school. It was also important for the head of year to hear Darren's rating of 8 and his mother's rating of 10 on the same scale. It suggested a motivation to try and make things work. Darren's commitment was rechecked throughout the sessions and remained at this high level.

The first two sessions focused on three main areas:
a) Exceptions.
b) Strategies for avoiding trouble.
c) Convincing teachers that Darren was serious about staying.

a) Exceptions

It was quite clear from the initial discussion that there had been some exceptions in Darren's behaviour during the past two weeks. These were explored with questions such as:

"What was different about these times? What else? What else?"

"When things were working, what was working?"

Darren was able to pinpoint several things which seemed to affect his behaviour positively: when teachers gave "good work"; that is, work he enjoyed, when he sat with pupils who didn't cause trouble, and if he himself felt "ready to work". Darren also indicated that he sometimes remembered to think about his behaviour although he often forgot, but that when he did think about it, his behaviour was better. However, at this stage he was unable to pinpoint any specific factors which made a difference. We therefore asked Darren to monitor the times he did remember to think about his behaviour to see if this would reveal any useful information. Darren recorded this on a chart which he sent to us after a week. This idea was also linked to a suggestion from the head of year about finding a "prompt" to help Darren remember. The head of year used a bracelet he wore to help him remember things - it was left to Darren to think of a way of his own. He came up with the idea of using his watch and asking Alex, his friend, to help him.

b) Strategies for avoiding trouble

During these initial meetings a clear picture emerged about the conflict Darren was experiencing between asserting himself amongst his peer group and conforming to the rules of the school. This was explored in great detail with the aim of helping Darren to develop strategies to avoid these difficulties. The ideas generated by Darren were summarised in a feedback letter sent to him after the second session. The attempt was to acknowledge the dilemmas and highlight the strategies formulated to help him deal with these difficult situations. It also included questions introducing further ideas. We termed Darren's avoidance of trouble a "quest" after he had told us about a game with a similar title that he enjoyed playing.

> "We talked about the need for something to change to con-vince the teachers you are serious about wanting to stay. This is not an easy quest. There are going to be a lot of tempta-tions for you to get into trouble, Darren, and you will have to find your strongest will power at times to be able to resist them. We looked at some of the things you could try:
>
> 1. In the corridor:
>   - walk away from trouble;
>   - find a teacher.
> 2. In lessons:
>   - sit with boys who are working;
>   - do your work - avoid arguments;
>   - ask the teacher or other pupils for help;
>   - put your hand up. (We thought this might surprise some teachers and wondered what their response might be).
> 3. Break time:
>   - go to your base room;
>   - don't hang around with boys who like trouble."

c) Convincing teachers that Darren was serious about staying
The school was beginning to lose confidence that Darren could improve. Something needed to change and the staff needed to see tan-gible proof of this. These ideas were again included in the letter to Darren, with the addition of a couple of questions which had occurred to us after the session had ended.

"We also wondered what else you could do for the teachers. One idea was either to talk to them or write a letter to explain what you are trying to do. The head of year thinks the teachers will take about two weeks to notice a difference in your behaviour, you think they will take a term. I wonder how long they will take and also how you will know that they have noticed a difference in your behaviour."

By the end of the first two sessions there seemed to be many indications that change could occur. Darren was motivated to try out the ideas and was receiving support from both his mother and the head of year. The discussions had been productive in high-lighting small but realistic actions Darren could take towards the goal of staying in school.

Crisis point!
The focus of the third session changed abruptly with the news that Darren had recently been involved in a fight and the school were recommending a permanent exclusion. Darren was clearly upset by the incident, in which he felt he had been provoked. The school was worried about the serious nature of the attack, and Darren's mother was confused and anxious about what was going to happen.

We first needed to redefine the goals. Darren and his mother stated clearly that they wanted him to stay at the school. The date for the governor's meeting had been set and hence their decision was outside our control. Darren he was on a knife edge and his behaviour would have to be exemplary in order to make an impression. We took a short break to give ourselves time to digest the new information and think about what would be most helpful.

In talking about the incident Darren had described a "mood" which seemed to descend on him in an uncontrollable way. Darren had mentioned this mood once in a previous session. At the time it had not seemed of central importance and exploring Darren's behaviour had taken up the meeting time. However, this now seemed to be a key issue and one which Darren wanted to talk about. We therefore asked Darren to consider two questions:

"How does the mood affect your life?"
"In what ways, if any, can you affect your mood?"

The intention was to help Darren begin to view this "mood" as something outside himself that he could assert control over. This approach, involving externalisation, can also help someone to view the problem afresh. Since the net is cast so widely, sometimes surprising effects of the problem in the life of the person and group can be considered, and, as a consequence, surprising exceptions can be discovered. Darren agreed to go away and think about the questions. He had been very subdued during the session and we sensed an enormous struggle between his desire to engage in new behaviour and the pressures of his peer group to continue in old ways. We hoped that we had managed to find the key to helping Darren achieve his aim of staying at school, but at this stage felt the situation might have reached too critical a point.

Final session
The exclusion had not been upheld and Darren was to remain in school. He had been given another chance and it was vital that we help Darren and his mother capitalise on this since they both wanted him to stay in the school. He had arrived armed with a comprehensive list of his thoughts about the questions we had asked. We were struck by how thoughtful he had been.

Darren's lists

Q1 How do my moods/behaviour affect my life?
    1. I am not getting a good education.
    2. I am inconveniencing my family by making my brother Den miss nursery and my mum by making her to come to meetings often. Also worrying all my family because they would like me to stay at school and have a good education. And myself by getting myself excluded and missing work and the school and the boy [i.e. the boy in the incident also missed school] because I have hurt another pupil.

3. My moods also affect my life by not having something I like i.e. science.

4. Setting a bad example for my brothers and sisters.

5. Also it affects me by having to go to meetings.

6. Because of my reputation, I often get the blame for things I have not done; and teachers are less likely to believe me when I am telling the truth.

Q2 In what way, if any, can you affect your moods?

1. Thinking about my actions before I do them.

2. By ignoring them (if trouble starts).

3. Talking about the incident to the person (reasoning).

4. If I'm egged on by my friends I would still reason with him or pull him aside then talk.

5. I can say to my friend if they are egging me on that there is no point in fighting because I will get kicked out of the school and he won't.

6. Look at the classroom procedures and obey them.

7. Ask if I can go and work with another teacher.

8. Sit with someone who I know is going to be good to work with.

9. To do all these things I will need someone to talk to who is here at the school all the time who I can go to if I feel I am going to get into trouble, this must be someone I trust (teacher).

Interestingly, the answers concern not only moods but also actions to avoid trouble. Much of the session was spent exploring these in more depth. A key issue for Darren seemed to be his ability to say no to "wind ups". He felt his response would be different depending on the size of the person doing the winding up, so the following graded responses were formulated:

- a little kid: Darren would simply tell him he was being cheeky.
- someone the same size: Darren would talk with him.
- a larger boy: Darren would simply walk away.

The discussion was extended to look at ways of helping Darren become an "expert" in wind-ups and several tasks were formulated asking Darren to observe what other people do in response to wind-ups and observe the successful ways he himself overcame them. It was agreed it might be useful if Darren practiced different ways, (for example, deflecting with a statement such as, "You're probably right"), on some of his family members (several cousins were volunteered for this practice).

This was our final session with Darren, although some contact was maintained with the school. A year later Darren is still in school. There have continued to be ups and downs, but he has managed to steer a course between sticking up for himself and keeping within the acceptable boundaries laid down by the school.

Katrina

Katrina attended an all girls' school and was referred at the age of 12. At an initial meeting with staff a list of concerns was given. Katrina was underachieving in her work and seemed to lack motivation; she was defiant to teachers, and had been taking things from home (such as toys) which she gave to others. I was also told that Katrina had recently been suspended from school because of the unacceptable level of her behaviour.

As part of the background information from school I was told that the head of year was beginning to think a residential school would be the best option, and that Katrina had for some time been seeing a peripatetic teacher (for emotional and behavioural problems) who was giving an informal counselling session once a week. Academically, Katrina was felt to be of at least average ability.

In answer to the question about what minimal changes the school would need to see for Katrina's behaviour to be acceptable, the teachers said she would have to be able to sit in a classroom and get on with her work, to be honest about her behaviour and to be able to talk about what was bothering her. I then enquired if there was any particular question the staff wanted an answer to: I was asked to assess whether Katrina was correctly placed at the school, or if some other institution might be more suitable.

In many cases, particularly involving young children, I might well meet all the concerned adults first. With an older student, especially if the student seems to be rejecting school, I might meet the student directly. These are not fixed rules, but rather rules-of-thumb. Students in such situations are often "reluctant" and a direct meeting can help build co-operation. With Katrina, before any kind of planning meeting took place, I decided to try out a direct one-to-one discussion.

Before meeting her I considered these issues: is Katrina concerned about what others say or not? What are Katrina's goals and has she clear ideas about them? Are there exceptions and what is being done? Does she like the present arrangements? I began with; "What do you think the school would want me to see you for?" She replied that it might be for "disrupting the class" and "back-chatting the teachers". I asked Katrina how she did this and was told, "by talking and saying things like 'so what'?"

Given her open honest answers, I asked directly, "Do you want to do this?" to which she replied, "I just do it ... it just happens". At this point it was difficult to judge whether or not Katrina was reluctant to see me and whether or not she cared about the situation. While I had any sort of co-operation I continued.

E.P: If you wanted to stop, would you be able to?

K: I think so."

I then explored the issue of whether she wanted to stay at this school. Interestingly, she said "very much so," and to a scaling question, with 10 equalling the maximum, instantly gave 10. I expressed my curiosity at her wanting so much to be in this school, yet hating some teachers and getting into so many difficulties. She immediately suggested, "I could try and stop". This seemed to indicate a decision to become a "customer" for a change. However, I was by no means sure. I therefore decided that it would be useful for me to stay "neutral" with regard to behaviour in school, and thought that I could most help Katrina by contemplating with her the two immediate alternative futures: one in which she chose to co-operate with the school, and one in which she rejected it. I momentarily asked about her will power to stop, which she told me she had, then asked about the effects of "trouble" on her life. She listed six effects, including her losing out on education, losing her friendship with her mother, being seen as a "naughty girl". The style of this questioning was very much influenced by White and Epston (1990). Though the question is clearly about the consequences of the problem, it is not problem focused in the sense of asking for details about the difficult behaviour and its possible cause. The whole interview was in fact influenced by the externalisation approach; we talked about the external problem which Katrina could decide to accept or not.

The next stage examined good things in the school and whether she knew of any exceptions to the problem pattern. Katrina described how she had "managed to avoid trouble during work" quite a few times, especially in science, and that she had felt good to be able to show improvements to the teachers. Although Katrina was not able to think of a time when she had completely resisted back-chatting to a teacher she remembered a time when she had done it less and had not gone too far. The result had been less trouble for her. Katrina was next asked, "If you choose a good path in school, how could the school help you?"

Katrina listed various suggestions, such as a once-a-week discussion with a teacher and a report back from her teachers about how things had been going. In fact, ordinary things on the whole being tried out by the school already. We finally discussed "signs of improvement" which would suggest she was changing, and how many days or weeks it would take before various adults would notice. Katrina listed "being good in lessons" and "working rather than talking" as the clearest signs that things were improving. Katrina felt it would only take a day for her to notice the difference but felt the teachers and her mother would take a little longer - perhaps two or three weeks. This disparity could have been related not so much to noticing the difference but the time it would take for the adults to believe that a change had really occurred.

Next, a planning meeting took place between myself, the head of year, and the special needs teacher (the parent had been invited but did not attend). We discussed the previously described strategies which the teachers agreed to put into practice. At the end of the same session we talked again to Katrina who agreed to work with the new head of year.

Katrina was deemed to have made improvements and was not brought to my attention as needing further casework. All that really happened with regard to "strategies" was that Katrina, of her own volition, decided to make use of them. What I believe was more important was that Katrina was able to consider her potential goals with an adult who did not try to persuade her to the "obvious" route of trying in school. This, I believe, sends a message of respect to the student, the attitude of respect for client choice being central to solution focused thinking.

Brian (why me?)

Brian (12 years old) was referred through an "inter service meeting" in a secondary school, a multi-disciplinary meeting where heads of year discuss pupils causing concern. Brian was described as lacking in motivation, poorly organised and frequently late for school. He had recently spent a disproportionate amount of time in B12 (a room allocated for pupils whose behaviour is deemed unacceptable by the class teacher). Brian had also systematically worked his way through the report systems in the school, finally having to report to the head teacher on a daily basis with comments from each subject teacher about his behaviour in class. Staff, however, could not observe any marked or consistent changes in Brian's behaviour and were at a loss as to what to do next. Brian's mother (Jean) had also written to the school outlining her frustration at Brian's difficult behaviour at home and his apparent lack of ability to take responsibility for his own actions.

Three meetings were held in school, each lasting approximately an hour, including a 5 minute break.

First meeting

The meeting began with everyone being asked in turn:
  "What would you like to take away from the meeting that would make you feel it had been worthwhile?"

This gave everyone the opportunity to speak at the very beginning of the meeting and encouraged a clear idea to everyone present about what each of their goals were. In contentious meetings it can also provide the opportunity to draw out similarities between the aims.

The responses largely focused on Brian receiving additional help in his learning and developing a more positive attitude towards himself and school. People often come to meetings with the notion of a solution residing in external support. Experience has shown the value of not getting locked immediately into a discussion (or a battle!) about resources, but rather to explore the effects or results of this "help". In the course of extending people's thinking to what would actually be done with the extra resource, it can high-light things which are already happening and the fact that they too can be a part of the solution.

Picking up on the phrase "more positive about school for more of the time", Brian was asked about the times when things were going well for him in school. He began by describing the days when he had "less control" over himself but was also able to report that 7/10 days were good days. When asked what was different about these good days, Brian described a positive sequence of events in which he felt good about himself, did his work and consequently made his teachers proud of him. Brian would sometimes know when he was going to have a good day because he would feel happier inside. In fact he felt he could be in a good mood most of the time but things would happen to stop this; for example, his brother would wind him up or he would be unfairly blamed in class by teachers. This led to quite a detailed discussion about what promoted a good mood and which ways Brian had found to maintain the momentum of this good mood. From Brian's answers it was apparent he felt external factors were very influential, particularly his perception of fair and unfair treatment. In situations perceived as unfair Brian would answer back to teachers and more often than not find himself back in B12.

At this stage Brian's mother, Jean, joined the discussion and described a series of events in Brian's life which had left him feeling victimised, including a serious accident after which Brian had to spend several periods in hospital. These preoccupied Brian to such an extent that it affected his sleep; he had become fearful and lacking in confidence and if anything happened it was used as further evidence that things were "stacked up against him". Brian and Jean further reported that they had sought help from a variety of different sources, including the child guidance service, but each time felt this was unhelpful because no-one had been able to give them a definite answer.

By the end of the session we had moved away from the initial focus of looking for exceptions in school to build on, and indeed it was difficult to see where the focus of change might be, given the mass of information. However, the latter part had provided a lot of rich information about Brian's beliefs and how these affected his life. In retrospect, it can be seen that Brian had given some clues right at the beginning, for example, that he felt he did not have control over what happened to him. The skill in solution focused thinking is to listen carefully for these clues.

The session ended with the suggestion of several tasks involving a combination of observing and doing.

- Observe the good things about school you would like to continue. This could provide information to consolidate.

- Observe when something bad happens and Brian doesn't get in a bad mood. This was designed to help Brian recognise times when he utilised strengths within himself to overcome a bad mood.

- Try and predict each morning whether the day will be a good one or a bad one, and see if you are right. Sometimes simply focusing your thoughts on something can change perceptions, in this case, that Brian himself could have some effect on what happened.

Second meeting
The second session was held a month later. Reflecting on our notes we decided to follow two themes which had emerged: Brian's view of himself as a victim and the need for an "explanation". This need, and how people can sometimes hold worse-scenario explanations about themselves, are discussed in detail by Furman and Ahola(1992). We began by asking, "What explanations do you have about why you are going through these difficulties?" Jean reiterated her views expressed at the previous session that Brian had lost confidence due to the accident and

feared he would fail to do as well as people expected him to. Brian initially found the question difficult. It was therefore rephrased (in solution focus therapy it is the therapist's responsibility to ensure they have been understood); "Can you describe one or two things which have been important to you?"

In describing the accident Brian referred to himself as "unlucky", the accident could have happened to the girl behind him but it happened to him. This helped to explain further Brian's feeling of being victimised by circumstances outside his control. I began to explore the notion of good luck and bad luck, but felt I was merely confirming for Brian his view of the world. So I decided to change direction, "What steps have you made to reclaim your life back from this bad luck?" The result was dramatic and illustrated for me the power of a question. Brian's mother immediately described him as a strong person who talked with people and that he had felt much better recently. At this stage I thought there were some firm foundations to build on. However, the conversation turned again to describing the fear and pain Brian faced. The need to find an explanation again emerged. This was explored through a sequence of questions:

"What difference would Brian's understanding make?"
"What difference would understanding why make?"
"If you could ask someone a question what would that question be?"
"Have you any ideas what the answer would be?"
"What difference would this answer make to your life?"

Brian replied, "I would get some of my confidence back". The word "back" hinted that it had been there before. Brian then high-lighted several differences in his life which would happen as a result of increased confidence. For example, "I would do more things, visit my aunt, I would think differently". An exploration of where Brian's confidence was at this point revealed that it was between a $1/4$ and a $1/2$ but he would like to see it at 1.

The session again ended with several tasks aimed at developing some of the ideas which had emerged during the discussion. For example, asking Brian to think about the things he did to help himself and to consider the areas of his life that the traumatic incidents had not affected. Brian was also asked to think about ways in which we could help him to understand why things had happened to him. The intention of these tasks was firstly to help Brian think about the times in his life when he was an active agent rather than a passive recipient of events, and secondly, to help us know what sort of explanation would make sense to Brian.

The final meeting

The final session was held three weeks later. Brian's mother did not attend but sent her permission for the interview to continue without her. The meeting opened immediately with a report from the school about the considerable improvements in Brian's behaviour resulting in the presentation of a merit certificate in assembly.

Several questions were used to high-light the factors which had been important and motivating in this change and to consolidate the strengths and skills which Brian had used. For example:

"What is different ?"

"What have these changes made in the way you think about yourself as a person?"

"Who else has noticed these changes?"

Brian talked about his worry that he would be "chucked out of the school", but also that he felt teachers were giving him more of a chance. He felt he himself had calmed down and commented with a smile, "For the first time I've found my will power. I like myself better".

The final part of the session explored what the next steps could be. Brian was keen to achieve another merit and also to improve his spelling. We talked briefly about how he could do this and the head of learning support agreed to develop this with him. At the end of the session we drew together the important changes which had occurred, emphasising that Brian was moving forward and noting how impressed we were with his will power to stop his life moving in one way and to go in another direction.

The head of learning support sent a letter to Brian's mother to feed-back on the session and to further encourage the positive changes which had occurred.

Dear Ms Brown,

I thought that I would write to give you a brief summary of the meeting Yasmin Ajmal, John Rhodes and I had today with Brian.

We were able to speak briefly with Mr Eagle (the head of year) before the meeting to find out how things have been in school since your last meeting with Yasmin Ajmal, Brian and I in May. We were all very pleased to hear that there has been a real improvement in Brian's behaviour and a positive change in his attitude and effort in many lessons.

Brian was clearly - and justifiably - pleased and happy with his progress. He described how he was now discovering skills and abilities that he did not know that he had. He was also clearly pleased that teachers in school and you at home had noticed his efforts.

The next steps identified by the school and Brian were for him to maintain this progress and try to improve on it. Brian felt confident that he would be able to do this. He said that if he had any difficulties he would like to be able to talk to Mr David. He also said that he would like to try and improve his spelling but felt that he could do this himself with some help from home.

We were all very impressed by the changes Brian has suc-ceeded in making - he deserves credit for this. We have not scheduled any further meetings at this point but, of course, if you would like to discuss anything please contact me at school.

Yours sincerely
Leslie Downing
Head of Learning Support

Final comments

Two months later Brian was still doing well and I met with him briefly. His whole manner had changed. He talked confidently about the strategies he used to make sure he didn't give up, and placed himself as an 8 on a scale where 10 denoted full confidence he could continue. He had valued the support he had received from his mother and the head teacher and felt the meetings had helped him with his thinking. I asked him what advice he would give to someone else in the same situation. He replied, "People can help you but you have got to help yourself".

I also learnt from the head of learning support about a minor incident in a class which one teacher felt was a sign that the old Brian was returning. The head of learning support checked with Brian who stated confidently he could sort it out and no further complaints were received.

Some general issues

In this last section we shall consider some general issues concerning solution focused casework in schools.

Assessment

Psychologists and others are quite often asked to carry out assessments on individual children. For example, a court might require information when dealing with a school non-attender. In solution focused work it is, perhaps, impossible to separate assessment from intervention. We have, therefore, not favoured a clear assessment phase followed by a phase in which interventions are recommended, as the classic problem-solving model suggests. That said, assessments of various kinds are possible and quite often information has been used for report writing from sessions such as those outlined in this chapter. For example, as well as describing problem behaviour, the report can also describe what works and what explanations are given by various participants. Durrant (1993) discusses the issue of assessment in detail.

Interventions

In the various original writings of solution focused therapists many interesting examples of interventions can be found. We have not, however, tended to use elaborate tasks and the suggestions made at the end of sessions have been very modest. The major intervention has been the interview itself (Tomm, 1989) with the emphasis on negotiating shared goals between the school and the student and exploring exceptions. The most common ending to our sessions is a series of compliments based on strengths and a specific focus on exceptions. Generally, we find that quite clear exceptions emerge in the majority of cases, and discussion, celebration, a refocus on these perhaps constitutes the solid core of our work. If there were no exceptions, then we would certainly give compliments and might suggest a formula task as described in chapter one such as, "Record those things about Joe which you would like him to continue doing in class". We have tended to use a problem focused question where we thought it necessary for maintaining co-operation: even then it is often only needed for a short period of time, and need not prevent a speedy return to solution oriented talk.

Concluding comments

Working with behavioural difficulties in schools is one of the most challenging areas of our work. People often reach a state when they don't know what else they can do and the situation is often presented in terms of failure. In supporting students, teachers and parents in their wish to change what is happening, we have found no model of approaching behavioural difficulties more useful and flexible than solution focused thinking. It enables a different story to be told, one which emphasises the skills, strengths and resources of the people involved. Furthermore, it is not an exclusive model and seems to combine successfully with other techniques.

Reading and spelling: Methods, motivation and interaction

The next two chapters will look at the use of solution focused approaches to reading and spelling. Chapter three is intended to provide a theoretical basis for our work. Chapter four will illustrate the techniques and approaches through a series of case studies and will also include further elaboration on some of the other methods that have been used.

Introduction

In the work of an educational psychologist, students are often encountered who, in spite of extra teaching, seem to be making no progress in their acquisition of reading skills. Many such children are found in the upper years of the junior school, but also throughout the secondary school. The focus of this chapter will be on the latter age group since it was with such students that solution focused ideas were first tried (Rhodes, 1993) and developed in a residential school for boys with emotional and behavioural difficulties. A small team was subsequently formed in our psychology service and this chapter reports on the joint work of the authors.

Through learning about solution focused therapy, it began to emerge that such ideas might be modified and used to develop interesting courses of action when applied to the situation of the student stuck in a pattern of apparent "no change". So, what contribution can solution focused thinking bring to reading difficulties? The following areas are highlighted:

a) What methods of learning and teaching actually work in any particular situation and how do you know?

b) What are the student's goals and motivation to learn? Likewise, what are the teacher's goals and motivation?

c) What is the interaction pattern of student, teacher and wider systems? Is there conflict or co-operation?

The rationale of the solution focused approach to reading will be examined under these three areas and comments made on relevant controversies. (For this discussion it will be assumed that a special needs teacher is working with a student.)

What methods of learning and teaching actually work and how do you know?

Many pupils who have experienced difficulties in acquiring reading and writing skills have developed a story about themselves as unsuccessful learners. However, it is true to say they have been active learners since birth (e.g. learning how to talk and to walk) and most have acquired some level of literacy. Looking at exceptions (i.e. what might have worked in the past or what is working a little in the present) can introduce a doubt into this view of zero learning and provide evidence of competence which can then be built on.

Examples of questions used could include:

"When did you make most progress in learning to read?"

"What were you doing at these times which was helpful to you?"

"How did you know you were making progress?"

"What helps most at the moment?"

The focus on successful learning can also lead to questions concerning other areas of the student's life, so we often begin in this way:

"What are your interests/hobbies?"

One student said he enjoyed football. This could have been further explored with questions such as:

"How did you learn this skill?"

"How do you know when you have learnt a movement well?"

"What told you you were getting better at this?"

"What does learning this tell you about yourself?"

Solution focused thinking naturally leads to questions about knowing how something is achieved; in cognitive psychology the ability of people to think about their own learning, memory, and so on, is termed "meta-cognition". Brown and Dehoache (1983) stated:

> "The basic skills of meta-cognition include predicting the consequences of an action or events, checking the results of one's own actions (did it work?), monitoring one's ongoing activity (how am I doing?), reality testing (does this make sense?), and a variety of other behaviours for co-ordinating and controlling deliberate attempts to learn and solve problems".

One implicit assumption of meta-cognition is that if individuals are more aware of their own thinking processes then their ability to learn and remember will be improved.

Some psychologists have attempted to develop a form of meta-cognitive training (Wright and Cashden, 1991), though the efficacy of this programme is still unclear. We have found the following questions useful and believe that such questions might well be one method of helping a student to develop and utilise a form of meta-cognition·

"How exactly do you learn to read and/or spell a word? Show me what you do."

"How do you learn to remember a word?"

"What is your best method of learning? What exactly do you do?"

"When you try to remember how to spell a word, what do you do? What are your thoughts?"

"Between now and the next time we meet, observe how you learn a word."

Since the focus of our interviews is very much on what works for a particular student, we find that there is no need to have a particular opinion about the best way of teaching reading in general. The first preference is always to build on the solutions generated by the student and teacher. We are, however, very interested by recent research in reading and would draw, for example, on the work summarised by Adams (1990). In particular, we have taken from Adams the idea that the teaching of reading (a) must use meaningful texts with well-written fiction and prose, and (b) also requires an explicit focus on orthography, i.e. the relationship between the spelling of English and its sounds. We therefore do not argue with teachers about "whole word" versus "phonic methods", but would hope for some flexibility on the teacher's part. This will be discussed again later.

The solution focused approach to reading is also neutral with regard to the concept of "dyslexia". That is, the proposition that some children have a specific difficulty with literacy, not accounted for by their general intelligence, and probably related to variance or deficit in a cognitive skill such as the ability to perceive sound patterns. In general, whether such a concept is useful depends on scientific research on groups of children; there does not yet seem a definitive answer. We tend to accept the position put forward by Bradley and Bryant (1985) that children with specific reading difficulties quite often have difficulties with phonology, that is, perceiving the sounds of English and relating these to the printed word. They argue that dyslexia is not an all or nothing category, but rather that children could be viewed along a continuum, with other dimensions also having relevance.

When parents say their child is "dyslexic" they are not usually interested in the scientific and statistical debate. They see their child struggling and want an explanation. Unfortunately, the label itself can take on unknown meanings for the child, and this is where solution focused questioning, particularly that which examines meaning, can be helpful. One young girl described herself as "dyslexic". When asked what that meant she replied that it meant that she could not read. She also added, "I'd like to be dyslexic, so I can tell my friends".

It seemed that she wanted an explanation to give her friends to account for her lack of progress. Being somewhat concerned about the negative implications of this construction, we suggested that dyslexia meant not that she wouldn't be able to read, but rather that we needed to find a "special method of learning" for her. This, of course, is one use of reframing, hence, in the solution focused approach we would try not to 'argue' with clients about the existence of dyslexia, but if necessary introduce new and more flexible meanings for the term.

What are the student's goals and motivation to learn? What are the teacher's goals and motivation?

As the title of this section suggests we need to find out the direction of change the pupil, teacher or parent would like to take and to help them decide on the first steps towards this.

Think of an activity you particularly dislike. For John Rhodes this might well be car maintenance, for Yasmin Ajmal it could be any form of DIY. Imagine having to do this day in day out, surrounded by others who seem to find it easy. Most adults would not tolerate such a situation and fairly extreme emotional reactions might well be the consequence. Typically these would range from anger to hopelessness.

Many young people find themselves in this situation at school with regard to the skills of reading and writing. It is therefore not surprising that an individual's belief in self, motivation and involvement in learning might become somewhat worn down.

Whether emotional difficulties are a cause or consequence of reading difficulties seems undecided by empirical studies. One piece of research (Porter and Rourke, 1985) found that 50% of children with reading difficulties did not have any particular emotional difficulties; the other 50% showed a mixture of depression, anxiety, aggression and somatic complaints. Butkowsky and Willows (1980) especially examined students' belief in their ability to learn to read and found lower expectations of success, a tendency to give up in the face of difficulties and the attribution to luck of any success. The conclusion from this research seems to be that students with reading difficulties do not necessarily have emotional problems (hence, this is not always the cause of their difficulties, though it might be for some), but a large number begin to have specific difficulties of motivation concerning reading. As stated at the beginning, this is hardly surprising; such emotions are normal responses.

Various psychologists have developed approaches which address these motivational and emotional factors. Lawrence (1973, 1985) demonstrated a form of simple counselling linked with a well-structured teaching programme. Using a cognitive-behavioural framework, Gentile and MacMillan (1987) suggested students with persistent failure engage in "fight or flight". Their teaching programme emphasises the following elements:

a) goal-setting.

b) self-incentives, that is, rewards chosen and given by the students to themselves.

c) self-monitoring, that is, students' need for very careful and detailed feedback on the progress they make, however small.

Other approaches have been used by psychologists, including the use of a family systems perspective. An example is given by Dowling and Osborne (1985) and an interesting one, using Ericksonian hypnosis, by Haley (1973). The systems approach, however, only seems to have been used with specific cases and does not appear to have developed into a regular approach used in the school setting.

Given the above, it would seem that the issue of motivation must in some way be addressed when working with a student who is not making progress with literacy. The solution focused framework seems ideally suited to this task by its attention to a person's goals and related beliefs and attitudes. The issue of motivation, goals and emotions are almost inseparable in practice. The following questions focus on these areas:

"Do you want to learn to read? Are you sure? Why is that?"

"On a scale from 1 to 10 where 10 equals 'I want to learn enormously' and 1 equals 'I don't care at all', where would you place yourself on this scale?"

"How much work are you willing to do? How much time will you spend on reading practice in the evening?"

"What will the first sign be that you are making progress in learning to read ?"

"In the future, when you can read, what kind of things will you be reading?"

"How will you finally know that you are a reader?"

Mere questions cannot create motivation from thin air, yet perhaps they can have various positive effects, including reminding a person of his or her deepest interests and hopes.

In practice, a simple classification of students' attitude to learning to read could be:

a) strongly motivated.

b) mixed motivation, that is, the student at the same time very much wants to learn, yet also feels hopeless, full of anger, anxiety and so on.

c) relative indifference, at least at the moment.

The questions seem to be very useful with the above since they are respectful of an individual's beliefs, do no harm to someone truly indifferent and even help them to reconsider their position. We believe that these types of questions respect a person's right to "self determination". Deci and Ryan (1985) have argued that a person's right to self determination is crucial in many spheres of activity. Their review of a great deal of experimental research suggests that people have far greater motivation for those activities they have freely chosen, and will have decreasing motivation for activities which are coerced.

Many students find themselves in the latter position with adults putting pressure on them to learn, for example, by lectures on the terrible things which happen to those who do not learn to read. With students who are "stuck", and even actively avoid engagement with learning, we believe it is important to emphasise their maturity and freedom to choose. This, we believe, can help them to rediscover their own motivation.

Several of the above questions elicit general goals. However, these can seem a long way off and the following questions are aimed at helping people identify the next step they can take to move in their chosen direction.

"Tell me what book (magazine, etc.) you could soon read which would tell you that you're making progress. And after that, which book?"

"On a scale of 1 to 10 where 1 describes someone who cannot read at all, and 10 is someone who reads really well, where would you place yourself on the scale now? What would you need to do that would tell you have moved to the next point on the scale? Who would be the first to notice? What would they notice? How would you know they had noticed?"

By a series of such a questions, "milestones" can be named and described which can become useful markers of progress for the student. In addition, very specific targets can be discussed; for example, the student could choose a list of spellings they would like to learn each week and practice these until "fluent" as described by Solity and Bull (1987). One student's list reflected his interest in football and consisted of the names of teams. The solution focused approach to reading uses goals in a similar way to Gentile and Macmillan (1987), yet emphasises the wider context and explores those goals which are meaningful to the student.

What is the interaction pattern of the student, teacher and wider systems?

In the first attempts to use solution focused thinking and methods with reading difficulties, most attention was given to the student, that is, the student's method of learning, motivation and goals. However, it soon become apparent that an equal attention was needed for the teacher's method of teaching, motivation and goals. Many teachers find it very painful to see their methods not working and feel that they are failing the student. Teachers can lose their motivation to teach and begin to feel hopeless. Hence, it is most important to ask the teacher questions such as:

"What methods of teaching have you found successful with this student? How did you know they were successful?"

"What has tended to work in the past? What were you doing differently at that time?"

"What would be a sign for you that the student is making progress? What would you see them doing?"

"What activities, books etc., has the student most enjoyed? What was it about those activities which interested the pupil?"

"Are there any ideas you have thought of but not yet tried?"

If a student is making little or no progress in working with a particular teacher, then that relationship can be conceived as a repeating, yet "stuck", interaction pattern. In some cases the participants seem to lose hope and think "nothing is happening". In other cases there is a more or less open conflict; the teacher might have excellent ideas and good motives yet the student may not see the benefit. In the ideal situation there is a "fit" of teacher and student goals, methods of learning/teaching, and mutual personal respect - and all this within their own social and institutional contexts.

In situations of conflict or apathy, the delivery of the curriculum can become very disorganised. There is little consistency of method or content, and any positive gains are not built upon. Hence, to use de Shazer's (1991) terminology, there will be exceptions but these will go unnoticed and be considered "flukes'". The issue of organisation over long periods of time is crucial for progress in literacy.

If a method is being used consistently, and yet does not seem to be working, then the solution focused perspective would suggest, "Try something different". In education there are often fierce debates about the "best way to teach". The solution focused approach suggests that we try different methods, and that whenever possible, we consult with students to see what they find useful and engaging. The issue must be: what works for this unique individual, at this moment in time, in this institution, within the context of my idiosyncratic constraints?

Besides developing a fixed interaction pattern with a teacher, the student might also have developed· specific patterns of interaction around the task of reading with other students and their family. White and Epston (1990) argue that the "life" of a problem sometimes needs a "life-support" system. To give a simple example, someone may continue to be afraid of public speaking, because they actively avoid all requests to speak in public. Such a person's employer might then stop asking the person to give talks and this in turn acts as a support for the problem. If a student is still in the mainstream at 14, and can hardly read, then it might well be that they have developed various strategies to help them "survive", yet these same strategies do not help the student to make progress. For example, after some progress, one girl said that her mother had refused to help her read some words on the TV, as she had done before in such situations. We have not made suggestions to students or teachers that they change such strategies, yet make them a focus of discussion by questions such as:

"What difference will learning to read make to your life (in school, at home)?"

"Who will be the first to notice? What will they notice? How will you know they have noticed?"

"How will this change their view of you? What does this tell you about yourself? How confident are you that you will be able to make progress? What will increase your confidence?"

Answers to these questions can be most surprising. One boy said his cat would notice before his sister (the boy was very distressed that his younger sister was ahead of him in reading).

The role of family members will, for some students, be a crucial aspect of their success or failure in learning to read. The focus of our work has been on older students in school, and issues of family interaction have tended to emerge indirectly, being very much left up to the student whether they wish to discuss such matters. With younger students (below 11 years of age), we believe more direct work with family members might be crucial and believe this could be an interesting future development.

Outline of the Solution Focused approach

The solution focused approach to literacy falls into three phases:

- solution focused interviews (with or without skills assessment)
- joint planning meeting
- reviews of progress

The rest of this section will give an account of these phases.

The Solution Focused interview

The three main areas of focus in this interview are those discussed in the last section, namely:

- methods of learning and teaching

- goals and motivation
- the social context and interactions

Each of these areas is explored by the use of questions as illustrated but in the actual situation there was much improvisation. There did not seem to be any particular order in which these areas should have been addressed. A flexible and general pattern is:

- a discussion of a pupil's strengths via talk of hobbies and interests
- focus on general goals (interests, work and possibly reading)
- specific focus on methods of learning, past success
- interactive issues, e.g. who will notice any improvements
- return to goals and specific targets.

During the planning stage, and during any feedback, it is sometimes interesting to use metaphors when communicating with a student, and even the teacher, particularly when a next step is being discussed. For example, one student when asked how he had learnt the skills of repairing cars used the phrase, "taking it apart and putting it back together". When discussing how he might set about acquiring literacy, the metaphor of his having been in, "first gear ... if not reverse!" was used and how in learning new words he could try taking them apart and putting them back together. Using a person's images, metaphors and phrases in communication does seem to make conversation more vivid, if only on the level of humour. With one student, a karate enthusiast, we spoke of "karate chopping" the problem.

The use of metaphors and stories is a feature of several therapeutic approaches, even perhaps an ancient and traditional way of suggesting new ideas and perspectives, as seen, for instance, in fairy tales. There is perhaps potential for more elaborate use, but that has not been an essential feature of our work. O'Hanlon (1987) gives a clear account of how Erickson used metaphors and stories. Often this approach involves making a story with parallels to the person's life, but in the story suggesting new endings, strategies, or developments.

Throughout the interview, there is an emphasis on a student's autonomy. First a student is asked by their teacher before the interview whether they would like to talk to someone about their reading; this voluntary assent is, we believe, crucial. Then at various points in the interview questions can be inserted such as, "Is it OK to ask these questions?" When discussing the importance of learning to read, it is useful not to be seen to be trying to persuade the student how essential literacy is; many people will have tried that. The question, "Why do you want to learn to read?", asked in a relaxed and friendly way, also shows respect for a person's self-determination. To emphasise the issue of autonomy most students were seen for the first time alone.

It is also essential to interview the teacher. Some possible questions were discussed in the previous section about the interaction between the student and the teacher. This interview was often shorter and simpler than the one with the student. The main topics covered are:
- successful methods already tried
- ideas the teacher has thought of but not yet tried
- knowledge the teacher may have about the pupils' learning style.

The interview with the teacher ranges from 20 to 40 minutes, and with the student from around 40 to 60 minutes. Session breaks are not used with the teachers, but sometimes with students. Compliments are used whenever is thought appropriate.

The planning meeting

The planning meeting could take place on the same day, or a few days later; a gap of some days seems useful, since this allows everyone to absorb the information and provides time for thinking and planning the next step. We invariably have the teacher and student together for this meeting. A fairly typical pattern for the meeting is:
- the interviewer reporting back on some aspect of the previous meeting, usually focusing on strengths
- again asking the student if they wish to participate and asking how much extra work they are willing to do, particularly in their own time
- a very detailed discussion of practical ideas. Who is to do what, when, how often and even where?

If the student or teacher has thought of some methods of learning or teaching, these are perhaps the best to use. It is, however, useful to have considered beforehand what teaching strategies could be suggested, and in general it seems useful for at least one "new" element to be added to that which was used before. In the manner of Furman and Ahola (1992), several ideas can be discussed and the participants then left to choose (some strategies are explained in a later section).

The review meeting

In line with other solution focused work (de Shazer 1988) there are two general directions in a review meeting:

1. If things are going well, recommend a continuation with or without some new ideas.

2. If no progress is being made, then new strategies are required or even a re-consideration of the original complaint.

If there are improvements these can be explored and built upon by questions such as:

"How did you achieve this?" (to the teacher and/or student).

"Who else has noticed? What will they have noticed?"

"What is the next step? What will the next sign of progress be?"

If the student has managed to learn specific words:

"How are you remembering these words?"

"How do you explain this?"

If specific "milestones" have been reached, then new ones can be discussed. Often teachers introduce changes to the original plans. These are accepted and why they had been useful is explored.

Usually the student and teacher are together at the meeting, but it can also be very useful to see the teacher alone to discuss details and anything they wish to say in private.

The time between the planning and review meeting varies enormously (from two to eight weeks). In general it seems wise to have a review meeting within a short time span if the situation is thought to be challenging, and then to review at whatever interval is thought to be useful. It is also helpful for a system of feedback to be set up between the teacher and the other people involved. For example, a card from the teacher indicating how things are going. This can help to encourage the teacher in situations of institutional chaos.

Assessment of skills and ability
It is not a necessary part of the solution focused approach to literacy to use extended and detailed "assessment", i.e. the use of tests to look at areas such as general or specific intelligence, reading and spelling levels. These tests are sometimes called "psychometrics". In fact, no direct assessment of reading and spelling needs to be carried out at all and several cases have been worked through successfully in this way. However, whether a skills assessment is carried out or not does not in general seem detrimental to a solution focused approach, except where it is thought likely that yet another assessment would upset or de-motivate a student. Most of these students have experienced many tests over the years, and the results are available in the thick files that have accumulated.

There is, of course, a much more general sense of "assessment" in terms of finding something out. In the latter sense "assessment" is interwoven with all the other activities of a solution focused approach and in fact it would be almost impossible to say which activities are strictly "assessment" and which are "interventions", the latter being defined as activities aimed at bringing about change. (The teacher may, of course, be carrying various kinds of informal assessment to help in the planning of the curriculum).

Concluding comments
In this chapter a basic introduction to a solution focused approach to reading has been outlined. The central issue of motivation in the context of the student/teacher relationship was discussed and questions which can be used to help people find what is motivating to them were high-lighted. Ways of establishing the best methods of learning for individual pupils were looked at and, most importantly, making these methods tangible and accessible to the students. In doing so the student's view of themselves as an unsuccessful learner may be challenged, which may allow new thinking for the student in terms of being an active learner. Consideration of the goals of the student and teacher has been

discussed as an important step in the process of negotiating an approach which works for both of them. Although certain key questions have been high-lighted, the skill lies in developing a series of questions to explore an interesting idea. Perhaps it is useful to think about it as a photograph which is being developed. The longer it is in the liquid (the longer you pursue a particular line of questioning), the more of the picture is revealed, until finally you have a clear image.

The solution focused approach to reading is not a theory of reading or teaching. Rather, it is a flexible theoretical framework for casework involving learning, and a creative set of questions and techniques which, at their best, may help participants to generate new ideas and think of new actions to try out. All the teaching strategies can be found in the literature, and certainly the general strategy of focusing on a goal is used in other approaches. The strength of the solution focused approach is that it seems to place all these diverse elements within a flexible framework and unifies them into one coherent way of working in difficult practical situations.

CHAPTER FOUR

How will you know when you are a reader?

The first part of this chapter will describe the application of a solution focused approach to literacy through a series of four case illustrations. In the second part the strategies we found to be particularly useful are summarised.

Illustrating the approach

Introduction

There are many types of reading and writing difficulties, due to a diverse range of disputed causes. Many children who fall behind their peers are picked up during their junior years and given appropriate help. Some students continue to have difficulties throughout their secondary school years. Those in a mainstream school can receive some form of extra help in class or on a withdrawal basis, provided by the permanent school staff or from a local peripatetic team of specialist teachers.

Some students seem to profit greatly from this extra teaching, others make very little progress, showing some of the more extreme reactions described by Gentile and MacMillan (1987) as "fight" or "flight". The former actively reject work and the latter seem despondent, to have given up. These are, of course, just crude labels. Many other ways could be found of describing young people's reactions, for example, "a sensible rejection of an inappropriate curriculum", or "temporary indifference due to competing alternative interests" or even "pedagogiphobia". Whatever the description, these young people are considered to be making insufficient progress in acquiring reading and writing, and usually somebody involved, student, teacher, or parent, is very concerned.

The main focus of our work has been with these students thought to be making little progress. These students were all working with an individual support teacher. To help clarify what our approach might look like, we decided to concentrate our efforts on two secondary schools. We met regularly so a method could be discussed, agreed and implemented. This chapter reports some results from this collaborative work and findings from earlier exploratory work.

Both schools are in Hackney: one is an all boys school in a multi-ethnic mainly working class area, the other is a multi-ethnic, co-educational school with a mixture of middle and working-class students. Our roles as educational psychologists involved a diverse range of tasks, including:

a) consultation and advice to staff

b) carrying out assessments

c) working directly with students, staff, and parents

The casework involved meetings with both individuals and groups. Educational psychologists very rarely have many meetings for any one particular case; the minimum number of meetings we held was three, and rarely extended beyond four. By practical necessity, educational psychologists' work in schools tends to be short-term, whatever their approach.

Case illustrations

The following section illustrates our work with four cases. Although the underlying structure for each case is very similar, the unique contribution of each individual is also high-lighted.

We begin with **Rupert,** an intelligent boy described as a loner. As the sessions unfold, we see him begin to find a direction and motivation, enabling him to begin to use his skills.

This is followed by **Elaine,** whose comments about not being able to read provide a rich personal view of her feelings and how her experiences have affected her.

Steven, the third case illustration, is a boy with general learning difficulties who found it difficult to articulate his views. The piece of work has two main phases: initially establishing some clear ways forward and setting up a pattern of working between Steven and his teacher; subsequently high-lighting, reinforcing and consolidating the changes which had occurred.

The final illustration describes working with two students, **Andrew** and **David**. It explores the notion of co-operative learning through the negotiation of shared targets.

Rupert

When I first met Rupert he was 12 years and 9 months old. In my "liaison meetings" with the Special Needs department I had been told that Rupert was only at a very early stage of reading and writing, yet in conversation seemed intelligent. He was receiving extra help, yet almost no progress had been made in the first year of the secondary school. I was also told that Rupert had an unusual and independent personality. He seemed to have almost no friends, was very withdrawn, and was very poorly dressed. In particular, his hair style was extraordinary, roughly the shape of a small mountain, rising almost a foot above his head. Since this was neither the accepted nor conventional fashion, his appearance provoked much abuse and commentary from others. Rupert, however, had stated to staff that he didn't care what others thought.

At the time arranged for me to meet Rupert, I heard a huge noise outside my room. When I looked out I found another student threatening to attack Rupert, several members of staff keeping the aggressor away from him, and a large crowd of student spectators. This carried on for some time, but eventually the other pupil was sent away and I sat down, though somewhat taken aback, with Rupert. I asked if he was alright and what had happened. He explained that the other student had sworn at him, so he had sworn back.

Given the difficult nature of this first meeting, and not sure if I should continue at all, I carried out a simple assessment of Rupert's skills and abilities in reading and spelling. Rupert was co-operative but extremely quiet. The tests placed him at an achievement level equivalent to that obtained on average by children at the end of their infant school.

The solution focused interview proper took place four days later. I felt that it was important to start by asking Rupert if he wished to work on his reading and spelling. On a scale of 1 to 10 he stated that his motivation was 8 (where 10 equals extremely interested). He later commented that he was more interested in spelling, but would work on his reading if it helped.

Rupert listed his interests as TV and short distance running. At school he liked geography, information technology, and "English a bit". On TV he liked cartoons, "Neighbours" and the "Adams Family". I asked him what jobs he would like to do in the future. First he said "dustbin man", then added an emphatic "no", and said the job was "dirty". He then stated that he would like to "make money" so he could "go to parties and discos".

To the question, "How do you learn best?" he made no clear answer. He explained that sometimes he did manage to "memorise" a word, and others times didn't. He added, however, that he was "good at facts and ideas", and when I asked, said he was willing to experiment with different ways of learning.

Rupert's first sign of progress was that he would be "better at his work". To clarify this I asked how he would know. After some thought he said he would begin to remember words like "because" which he had difficulty with and "words I don't see much". Again he said he wasn't very interested in reading but in the future thought he might read comedies.

I next had a short meeting with his teacher, Joan. She explained that whether he worked or not depended on the subject and in general little progress was being made. She had taught him for a year in a small group and also worked with him in class. In the small group they had undertaken diverse kinds of work, for example, looking at sound-spelling patterns and using "look, cover, and say" for spelling. She stated that a first sign of progress would be to "see him using words from the special needs department in other subjects", and for there to be "improvements across the curriculum", for example, Rupert showing signs of involvement and pleasure.

Planning the work

After my first meeting with Rupert, I went away thinking that it had not been very successful. It is difficult to convey in print how Rupert inter- acts; he almost never smiles, and says little. It was therefore difficult to know whether he had thought our discussion worthwhile. His interests seemed to me so minimal that I could not think how we could use these to construct an interesting programme of study.

Interestingly, I discussed this case with a friend who stated bluntly (as only a friend can) that I had allowed my own prejudice in not liking tele- vision to get in the way. It was pointed out how many questions could have been asked. For example, what do you like about TV?, why?, and so on. Inspired by this, I arranged a very short meeting with Rupert before the next joint meeting.

After some preliminary discussion about work that week, I asked him a series of questions about his interest in TV. To the question, "What do you like about TV?", he replied, "It's different from real life". Eventually we began discussing the possibilities of writing a "thriller" and even a "TV script".

At the joint meeting, the TV script idea was discussed with Joan who became very interested, adding that drama was one of her special inter- ests. We conceived the idea of doing a "story-board" or at least a series of pictures with narrative. We next planned some spelling work which Rupert was to take home. The exact details of the new work were mapped on a timetable. The spellings were to come from a book on spelling patterns, and the rest from his writing.

The review meetings

There were two review meetings: one after 2 months, the other after 7 months, at the end of the school year.

Joan stated that there had been several improvements. Rupert was co-operating better with his teachers, and two teachers had actually spontaneously commented on Rupert's more motivated approach to his work. Joan also felt her relationship with Rupert had become more relaxed and cited as an example an occasion when Rupert had giggled and played a joke.

Rupert had shown interest in the work. The story-board had been completed, but had not been very developed. Most successful was the use of a book; Joan had given him a choice of four short novels, and Rupert had chosen a young person's version of "The Elephant Man". Each week they read some of this and then five spellings were taken home, based on any words found difficult. They had informal discussions on spelling patterns such as thinking up words ending in "ible" (this is based on an idea of Bryant and Bradley, 1985). A few days later the words were tested and Rupert was spelling about 4 out of 5 correctly. He was receiving 50 minutes one-to-one teaching per week, plus some small group work.

We decided to carry on, adding that a possible next step would be for Rupert to write his own story. A week later I received a letter hand-written by Rupert listing some words he had learnt to spell.

Dear John,

How are you? Here are the spelling words that you wanted to know about. The words I have learnt are:
Chapter 1: enormous, interesting, horrible, ugly.
Chapter 2: hospital, creature, usually.

I also learnt: terrible, incredible, impossible, famous, eventually, finally.

See you soon,

From Rupert.

I sent him a short reply.

Dear Rupert,

I was really pleased to get your letter. I was very impressed with the words you have learnt. They are very difficult.
Hope you're enjoying the story you're reading.

Seen any good T.V. recently?

See you soon,

Yours sincerely,

John Rhodes.

At the last meeting more developments were noted. Rupert had continued to work and in history had participated for two days in a three day play. Previously Rupert would not have participated at all and as such his involvement suggested an important change. Joan stated that he now "relates to me". However, it was of particular interest that Rupert had written two short accounts of recent visits, and, a month after finishing "The Elephant Man" had retold the story to Joan. She wrote this down, the whole adding up to 4 sides of A4. Watching her writing, at one point he asked, "Are those speech marks?". Later in private, Joan pointed out an intriguing part of his retelling, as follows: "The coach driver helped them off. The doctor said: 'Nurse come and help me'. Once they go into a room, Dr Treves pulled off the cloth on his head. The nurse screamed, Dr Treves said: 'Be quiet'. Dr Treves went and asked Merrick, 'Can you read?' Merrick said 'A little bit'. Dr Treves gave him a book. It was a Roald Dahl book. It was called 'The Champion of the World'. One week later and the hospital administration went and wrote to The Times about Merrick and how they needed money to keep him in the hospital."

I found this very moving. Joan was well aware of the possible social analogies in this story, but at no time were these commented on.

When I asked Rupert in the meeting how he was learning words, he replied, "I look", adding that this varied from 1 to 2 minutes. When asked if he had noted improvements he stated: "I can write down more words in less time." When asked how, he replied: "I know the words and don't have to ask the teacher all the time".

Subsequent testing revealed Rupert had made 2 years and 2 months progress in reading and 3 years and 5 months in spelling over an 8 month period. I was very surprised and very pleased.

Elaine

Elaine was said by the school to be intelligent and friendly, yet was making very little progress in reading, having reached the age of 14 with a reading age test score of approximately 7 years. Taking this at face value, it seemed that she had not made any measurable progress for several years. Having gone through the "Statementing" process (i.e. the process whereby a local education authority requests assessments and then provides additional resources to meet the needs of the student, such as an extra teacher), Elaine was receiving 9 hours extra help per week from a support teacher, a mixture of in-class support and withdrawal work. The teacher reported that Elaine seemed unmotivated and was often disorganised, losing books or forgetting them. Her mother was said to be "horrified" at Elaine's lack of progress. In response to a question about the first signs of progress the teacher talked about Elaine coming into class and discussing a book she was reading. Another indication for the teacher that Elaine was feeling happier about her reading would be if she spontaneously went to the book shelves and chose a book for herself.

Elaine proved to be very open and showed intelligence in her answers. On a scale of 1 to 10, where 10 equals a maximum motivation to learn to read she gave herself a 10. In answer to the question about why she wanted to learn to read she answered, "I don't feel independent", and later, "I don't feel like a person." Final proof for her of learning to read was to "pick up any book I want to read." We broke this down into a series of milestones:

- "Just 17" (a magazine for teenagers)
- novels by Judy Bloom
- "Flowers in the Attic" by Virginia Andrews
- texts in her history and literature lessons.

Many questions were raised: how she best learnt, ways of finding this out, and what difference reading would make to her life. To the last question she replied, "I could teach my kids, if I'm looking for a house I would be able to read the signs, and I would be able to read adverts and notices in shop windows." These were very practical and painted a very clear picture of how important the skill of reading is to be able to function effectively in life. Elaine wasn't sure about how she learnt a word but stated she didn't find saying the sounds in her head particularly useful because, "some words I can't pronounce".

A week later at a strategy meeting we discussed experimenting with different ways of learning how to read new words. Elaine had overheard on the bus two children discussing "phonics" and she said she wanted to learn some of these. This was curious in the light of our previous discussion about letter sounds, but I made no comment. We agreed to set up three methods of learning to read words:

a) a method of just looking

b) sounding out letters

c) saying letter names

She was to be tested on the words she had learnt once a week at school. All previous good work was to be continued, except "flash cards", which Elaine had said she didn't like. Even though the teacher had thought these useful, given the range of other approaches being used it seemed unnecessary to use them and important to respect Elaine's wishes. It was unlikely that Elaine would persevere with something she did not like.

At the review meeting four months later substantial improvements were reported. The teacher commented that there had been a "huge jump" in confidence, work done, and texts attempted. Elaine herself said, "I can read almost anything". She was still, of course, very much behind her peer group, yet was seeing that she could attempt most texts, even if she did not know all the words. Additionally the teacher's signs, of progress had occurred; Elaine had entered her room and spontaneously chosen a book to read. I asked about what difference better reading made to her. Elaine talked about how she was able to "have a go at my school work myself rather than getting my friends to read it for me". She was also able to read the teletext, whereas previously her mother had to do this for her. It seemed as if Elaine had already found some of the independence she had mentioned in our first interview.

Elaine now wanted to stop using "Just 17" as her measure of progress, preferring to do something useful for school. She and her teachers were going to choose an editorial from a newspaper such as The Independent. At this meeting Elaine also said that her next sign of progress would be attempting Shakespeare. I must have looked surprised since the two teachers informed me that this would be useful as it was a necessary part of the curriculum. (Interestingly, this was clearly remembered as a significant turning point by Elaine over a year later in a follow up evaluation interview).

At the last meeting I repeated the tests I had previously used with Elaine. Instead of staying at a fixed reading age level of 7, she was now making progress at the same rate as chronological time (that is, over a year-long period was making a year's progress according to the test norms).

Steven

Steven was in his first year at secondary school when he joined the project. He had a statement of special educational needs and received at this time additional support from a teacher (Leila). He was described as a boy with general learning difficulties who was greatly lacking in confidence, and there were concerns about whether he could cope with the demands of a curriculum at a secondary school level.

First Session

The first meeting was held with Steven and Leila. Steven was very shy during the interview and often indicated difficulty in answering a question by shaking his head and looking at the floor. However, there were some questions which Steven could answer and it proved helpful to continually re-phrase questions until he felt comfortable in answering.

Steven was definite that he was more concerned about his spelling than his reading. He then proceeded to place himself at 7/8 on a spelling scale where 10 is a very good speller. This was surprising but accepted as his rating. Steven said he would like to reach 10.

"How will you know when you have reached a 9?"

Steven said he would be able to write in a neater way with joined-up letters and with proper spaces between words. Although handwriting style is not necessarily the most important part of spelling, Steven had revealed that the appearance of his work was very important to him and on this basis it was a valid goal. Additionally, he would only make 5-6 mistakes on a page as opposed to the 9 mistakes he thought he was making at the time.

I decided to follow this up with a question exploring how others would view Steven, as I was curious about the importance he placed on the look of his work.

"Who would be the first to notice you had reached a 9 in spelling ?"

Steven paused and said it would be his Humanities teacher.

"How will you know she has noticed?"

Again Steven thought hard and felt she would come over and talk about his work with him. This led to a discussion about other teachers and how important it is to Steven that he knows when he has done well. Having established this it was agreed that his support teacher would mention it to his teachers and Steven would report back to her any comments he had received.

I returned again to the first question in this sequence. The solution focused approach emphasises the value of exploring useful areas in depth to establish the maximum amount of information.

"Who else might notice you have reached a 9?"

Steven thought some of his friends would notice, particularly James who was in his form.

"How confident are you that these people you've talked about will notice the improvements?"

Steven stated clearly that he was very confident. Leila said she thought it could possibly happen. I used this difference between their predictions as the basis for asking Steven what he knew about himself that made him confident. Steven replied, "I will work harder".

Steven found it quite difficult to think about any strategies he used to help him learn a new word. However, a series of detailed questions revealed he did have some ideas, but that he did not use them systematically. Among the questions designed to help Steven think through the stages he used were:

"What is the first thing you do when you are learning how to spell a new word?"

"When you have done this what do you do next ?"

"How do you do this? Tell me exactly what you do."

"How do you help yourself do this?"

This information was then used to devise a programme using Steven as the "consultant". It took a while but was more meaningful because it had been devised by Steven himself.

In his reading Steven placed himself as an 8 on a scale where 10 is a very good reader. He would know he had improved when he could read "harder" books. This opened up an interesting discussion about how we know when a book is hard resulting in the following classification system:

- easy books: Steven can read them
- fairly hard books: Steven would find some words difficult
- hard books: books with a lot of difficult words

This not only encouraged a "staged" approach towards Steven's goal of reading a hard book, but also encouraged him to evaluate what he was reading.

Steven said he would improve his reading if he read more. This was developed through the following questions:

"How often would that need to be?"

"When is the best time to read?"

"Who will you read to?"

Steven thought every day might be too much if he wanted to go out and play, but he would try and read when he got in from school on most days.

The session ended with a comment from Leila that she had not heard Steven talk so openly or in such a committed way about his learning. This was encouraging for me to hear as I had found it hard going!

Second Session (6 weeks later)

Leila opened immediately with a comment that she had noticed several marked changes in Steven over the past few weeks. Steven preferred that Leila should talk about these and smiled as she spoke. Leila outlined the following:

- Steven was approaching his work with much more confidence and was keen to try for himself first before asking for help.

- Several teachers had commented about this and Steven had received five merit certificates for an "excellent attitude". I asked what this meant and was told: working hard and being interested.

- Steven had learnt sixteen words. If he couldn't write a word he would try again but if he still couldn't do it he would choose to leave it.

- Steven commented that Leila had sometimes forgotten to help him with his work. He agreed to remind her - another important step in Steven taking responsibility for his learning.

- Steven was reading every other day. He had chosen to read to his young nephew of a few months old and, judging by the beam on Steven's face, this was a very popular activity.

I asked Steven and Leila what had made the difference. Steven again deferred to Leila to answer. It is not always easy to know how to approach a student who is reluctant to talk. However, I could have tried the following question which is sometimes used: "I reckon you feel (the person) will be able to present your view well - but feel free to add any further comment." This respects the pupil's choice and also offers an open invitation to comment. Leila high-lighted that both Steven and herself were much clearer about the goals they were trying to achieve. The first meeting had helped them to focus their time together and Leila felt the relationship between her and Steven had become more equal in that Steven now wanted to learn as much as she wanted him to. An important aspect of this was that Steven was taking more responsibility for his learning.

Final Session

We met six weeks later. The improvements in Steven's confidence had continued and he was still having a go for himself in class. Steven was also gaining enormous pleasure from reading to his nephew. This confirmed the importance of finding something which is motivating for a particular individual. It also illustrates research on intrinsic motivation (Deci and Ryan, 1985) which suggests that activities which are self-motivating require little external maintenance.

Steven had read a "harder" book with Leila and commented that he now thought it was easy because he could read it. This was an interesting point - that books would change classification according to how easily Steven could read them. Leila also commented that she had heard Steven talk about books using his classification system to some other boys in his form, which suggested it had been a good and understandable system for him.

Both Steven and Leila reported that they felt the project had been very helpful and Steven thought he had reached his targets. Steven had achieved a measure of success which had surprised him and he had discovered a number of skills he had not thought he possessed.

For Leila the project had introduced a way of working with pupils which fitted her style and approach. She liked the tangible proof of progress that the clear targets provided and felt that because of their practicality they had been relevant to everyday lessons. In addition, she had become enormously curious about the ways Steven learnt and felt she now knew what to ask him.

Postscript

Two months later at an Annual Review (a statutory meeting held once a year for all pupils with a statement for special educational needs) Steven's progress was reported to have continued. He was now working with a different support teacher and had managed the transition very well. Furthermore, he was still reading to his nephew!

Working together - a peer tutoring approach

The impetus for using a peer tutoring approach as part of the reading project came through a discussion with the head of learning support in a secondary school. She was concerned about two year-7 pupils, David and Andrew, whose difficulties with reading and writing were affecting their work across all the curriculum areas. It also emerged that they were friends who often worked together in class.

Peer tutoring as an approach has been widely researched (Topping 1987). Although results vary and criticisms are levelled at research methods, general conclusions indicate the approach can have enormous benefits on the progress and understanding of pupils. Furthermore, it utilises a very rich resource present in all schools - the pupils themselves. Essentially, it consists of asking two pupils to work together, where one reads or does a specific academic task, and the other acts as a 'teacher' by listening and helping.

What do we want to learn? How do we learn best?

Much of the initial part of the first meeting centred around a scaling question:

"On a scale of 1 to 10 where 1 is no good at all and 10 is very good, where would you place yourself on the scale for reading/spelling?"

David rated himself as a 3 in spelling and a 4 in reading. Andrew thought he was a 4 in both cases. It was significant they did not place themselves at a 1 on either scale. Although not explored in the interview, a pupil's rating of themself can lead to a rich discussion about the skills they have already achieved to reach that point. For example:

"What things can you already do that make you confident you are a 4? What else? What else?"

The answers can provide a foundation on which further skills are developed in addition to underlining for the student the progress already made.

The scaling question can be developed in different ways. Here are two examples of questions used which establish clear targets to work towards:

"If you are a 4 now on the spelling scale, how would you know you had reached 5?"

For David the ability to spell long words (of 7 to 8 letters) would be a sign to him that he had moved to the next point. Later in the interview he identified a list of specific words, for example, "Arsenal" and "technology", which would fulfil this criterion.

"What would be the first sign of progress in your reading?"

For Andrew, a tangible sign of progress would be the ability to read a word in science his teacher did not expect him to know. And how would he know the teacher had noticed? She would tell him.

Further to this Andrew thought he would improve by reading regularly and immediately commented that he read the Bible every evening with his mother. It seemed as if he had suddenly made the connection between an activity he was already carrying out and a way he had identified as being helpful. A key feature of the solution focused approach is to encourage people to continue doing what works.

Andrew's response to the following question was also interesting:

"What difference would improving your reading make to your life?"

He stated he would read the signposts when he went walking, thus relating the activity of reading to one of his hobbies, which was both meaningful and motivating.

The next phase of the interview explored the best method for learning new words.

"What exactly do you do when you learn a word?"

"How do you learn to remember a word?"

Both Andrew and David described a number of strategies they used, including using sounds, covering up words, copying words out. When using sounds David also commented that he preferred to do this in his head as he easily felt embarrassed. This was an important piece of information and could have implications for the teaching approach used with David; if he felt embarrassed saying sounds out loud it would be counter-productive to make him do this. It also raised the question about the ways he could use this strategy effectively in his head.

At the end of the meeting the boys agreed to look closely again at the methods they used. The purpose was both to validate their successful approaches and reinforce their thoughts about how they learnt.

How was the information used?

Using the information gained from the initial meeting, the head of learning support devised a programme of work in collaboration with the boys. She had particularly liked the scaling question which she felt led to very practical personal objectives. The programme involved both reading and spelling and included a time for the boys to discuss the strategies they were using, thus reinforcing and extending their methods and understanding of what they were doing. The learning programme will not be outlined in detail here. However, there are one or two parts worth noting, as the programme brought together, as a basis, the learning strategies outlined by the boys and also introduced other ideas.

- The boys selected a bullseye chart and decided they could fill in a part of this once they were able to spell a word on two consecutive sessions.

- An achievement scale was devised on which the boys would record if they felt they had improved. This actually developed, through use, into a self monitoring scale for recording how well they thought they were doing.

- The boys arranged to meet each day before lunch to help each other with their spelling.

-The head of learning support met with the boys once a week to discuss how they were doing and plan the next steps.

Evaluation

After 10 weeks David and Andrew had learnt 40 words, completely filling their bullseye chart, and were keen to start another. They had also asked to extend the motivation scale beyond 10 to include 11 and 12!

The teacher reported enthusiastically about how the project was developing. Both the boys were keen to learn their spellings each week and were excited about the prospect of filling in sections of the bullseye chart. The teacher felt that healthy competition was providing a strong motivation to continue while not detracting from the gains the boys were experiencing working together on a joint project. The teacher also commented that as her work with the boys developed she was becoming more and more interested in finding out their views on what they were doing. She felt the questions derived from the solution focused approach had given her both the confidence and the tools to do this.

Strategies

In this section the various kinds of strategies for teaching will be summarised and reviewed. These fall into two very broad categories:

1) specific methods borrowed from other well-known approaches to teaching literacy

2) general ideas inspired by or borrowed from the whole range of solution focused thinkers

For specific methods, as previously stated, we have been quite willing to borrow from any of the major approaches known to us. Two extremes are:

- the "learning-to-objectives" approach, that is, where a specific target is given, practiced and tested until mastered (see Solity and Bull, 1987).

- the "apprenticeship" or "real book" approach; for example, as described in the work of Kohl (1973) and given momentum by Smith (1971). This emphasises using published books of "real" authors (as opposed to anonymous reading schemes), a student's own interests, motivation, and creative activities. Thus language competencies (e.g. phonics) are developed within a meaningful context.

We have not used long and detailed "phonic" programmes, but might do so if we thought it appropriate. A development of sound/symbol awareness has often played some role (Bryant and Bradley 1985); we have often suggested practice with spelling as another way of strengthening orthographic awareness. (The relevance of spelling to reading is discussed by Adams, 1990).

The general ideas inspired by solution focused thinking are as follows:

a) Experiments
The student and teacher can be asked to experiment with three methods of learning to read or spell specific word lists. For example, three sets of 10 spellings can be given, one per week, and each learnt in a different manner. The aim is not to conduct a controlled experiment, but to find a method which seems to work for the moment, for this student. As important as the result might be, the implicit and sometimes explicit message is: you have your own, "best method", and "you can use the method you like best".

b) Noticing Tasks
Student or teachers can be asked, "Notice how you best learn" or, "Notice what you do when you learn a word/phrase/text." This encourages people to reflect on what they are doing. The implicit message is that the student is already doing something which is helpful to them, such as having the skill to learn competently - we just need to find out what these skills are. This may sound very obvious, but our experience of students with persistent difficulties is that they often view themselves at the lower end of a continuum of "can't read - can read" and do not think they possess the skills to move away from that position.

c) Milestones
In the initial meeting, or planning meeting, significant "milestone" texts can be negotiated. It is difficult to imagine how the task of learning to

read must appear to those working with almost no progress, an endless sea with no land in sight? Feelings of panic, of drowning, and getting no-where? By asking questions such as, "Reading which book next would show you're making progress?", " And then which book ?", "What would finally prove to you that you are a reader?" and "What book or magazine or whatever would you be reading?", the student can be given a kind of overview or map of the task ahead, and interestingly the task then seems more manageable.

Not all students give clear answers, but some can even name exact titles and authors; it is as though seeing others read a specific book has symbolised their own lack of success.

d) Do Something Different
The "Do something different" task, as explained in chapter one, is used in situations where repetition of a "solution" or method has not led to success (de Shazer,1985). In the planning meeting it is worth considering the range of methods used so far and to try to suggest at least one new element, however modest. Sometimes this can be a simple switch of focus, for example, from "reading" to "spelling", from reading aloud to silent reading. Alternatively, one can find a book the pupil enjoys to use as a resource for teaching language competencies (e.g. phonics, focusing on whole words). Whatever the suggestions it is important they fit with the conceptual framework used by the teachers involved.

Concluding comments
The strength of the solution focused approach to reading and spelling is that it seems to unify and co-ordinate many diverse ideas and practices which experience and research suggest are useful and empowering. It is not a new approach to teaching reading, but rather a flexible and creative way of doing casework with literacy in school and community settings. Nor is this approach just "therapy" as extra counselling would be, since it also suggests ideas for the very technical aspects of learning and teaching. Rather, we would prefer to see this approach as one example of the general activity of solution focused thinking. A next interesting step might be to look at how these ideas could be used with

younger children, particularly where their family members wish to become involved.

The focus of our work has been the acquisition of literacy. However, it would seem quite feasible to apply these ideas to any situation where little progress is being made in the learning of a skill, and motivation is becoming problematic, from number work to persistent motor driving test failure. Perhaps we should re-name this method as a solution focused approach to learning and skills acquisition.

We have not yet carried out any statistical analysis of our work which we see as a first phase of exploration. Clearly, there are multiple factors and elements involved in a solution focused approach and these would make considerable demands on any research or evaluation design. Our direct experience, and the testimony of those involved, suggest, however, that it is a very useful and interesting addition to our ways of working with unique individuals struggling with literacy.

CHAPTER FIVE

Consultation:
Creative dialogue with teachers

This chapter will look at the use of solution focused thinking in consultation with teachers. Consultation is a widely used term and the distinction between consultation, casework and project work in schools is often a blurred one. For the purposes of our work we use the following definitions:

Consultation: work involving individual discussions with teachers about a range of issues, usually concerning individual students or organisational issues such as classroom management. A typical aim of such a discussion is problem solving. However, there may be other purposes such as seeking information.

Casework: work involving individual discussions with teachers and direct contact with students and parents.

Project Work: work involving consultation and participation in a system, for example, discussions about a class and such further involvement as classroom observation or attending a staff meeting.

We recognise that these distinctions are simplistic - in reality our work may span one or more areas, with consultation used as thread to link the activities together.

During regular visits to schools, educational psychologists are often asked, sometimes at short notice, to consult with teachers about issues such as individual students, classroom management and work with parents. Ideally, consultation should take place in a calm atmosphere, with sufficient time for a detailed discussion and ample opportunities for follow-up. And this is in fact the way we work in some schools, for some cases. However, time in school is a precious commodity and within the context of receding resources and no cover for classes, there is often only the span of a break time or, if lucky, an assembly period to discuss an issue. These time constraints are far from ideal and yet often seem unavoidable given the busy nature of schools. In this situation, the teacher may feel driven to give a rapid account of the problem and its details, which allows little time for more creative collaboration. Furthermore, the expectations of the teacher, whether for advice, referral for extra services or problem solving, might not be clear.

It is within this context that the value of using a solution focused approach has been explored. It does not provide specific answers but what it does offer is a structure to help people clarify their goals and put together solutions in small achievable steps.

The key elements of a Solution Focused approach to consultation

Having reflected on our work, we would suggest that the following are the essential elements or thoughts a consultant must keep in mind throughout an interview:

- What are the expectations of those involved? In particular, what would the consultee like to achieve within the session?

- What goal does the consultee hold for the student or for the problem situation? What might the student's goal be?

- What beliefs or attitudes does the consultee have towards attempting to solve the problem? For example, does the consultee wish to try out new actions or not?

- Which strategies are working already?

- What are the exceptions to the problem pattern?

Not all these areas will be explicitly addressed in an interview; rather, the above represent a sort of map which can guide the consultant in the choice of which direction to follow. The first three areas are perhaps the most important for the consultant to consider, with the last two coming into play as the consultation proceeds.

The following case illustrations high-light some of the most useful questions and processes.

Sarah

> "I've got a really good but inexperienced teacher who feels it is all going wrong in her class and doesn't know what to do. Can you talk with her?"

The inexperienced teacher, referred to by her head teacher, was Sarah. Although she had only been at the school a relatively short time Sarah was highly valued by the head teacher who was concerned about how demoralised she was feeling.

Sarah was released to talk with me for half an hour. She spoke immediately of a small group of very difficult students in her class and a number of others who were potentially volatile. Until recently she had employed a number of successful strategies to handle the difficult students and keep the class stable. She had drawn on the support of the rest of the class to help her in this but now felt this source of support had gone and none of the strategies she had previously used successfully seemed to be working. She was also concerned that too many students had been commenting, "It's not fair, nothing happens" in relation to the behaviour of the difficult students.

While Sarah was talking I listened carefully to what her description revealed about her style of teaching and approaches to classroom management, which is always potentially useful in later discussions. For example, Sarah mentioned how she liked to talk with students about what she was doing and was interested in their viewpoints.

A key feature of solution focused therapy is the negotiation of workable goals; it is important to focus on a small but realistic step. This can sometimes be identified by an opening question, "What would you like to take away from this discussion that would make you feel it had been worthwhile?" Sarah's reply, "I just don't know", suggested, however, that she could be finding it difficult to see a time when the problem would not exist. This made her feel helpless and de-skilled. O'Hanlon and Weiner-Davis (1989) describe how clients who are overwhelmed by their difficulties frequently lose sight of their problem solving strengths.

At this point, I offered her a choice of two further questions, both designed to work towards a goal, as I was unclear which would be the most helpful:

"What would be the first sign of progress?"

"Imagine it's a month's time and the class is operating as you would like it to. What would be happening?"

Sarah chose to answer the second question and began with an interesting phrase: "Well ... they will have moved two levels nearer to what I want." In this way she naturally described the process in terms of a scale. She described her class as a 2 on a scale of 1 to 5 where 1 is a riotous class and 5 is a textbook class. She wanted to see them at 4.

Sarah was now able to consider what the class would be doing differently in order for them to move up the scale. In subsequent questions I re-used Sarah's phrase "moved up two levels". As this was how she had refered to the situation it seemed to make the communication more meaningful. She high-lighted three areas:

a) students being on task

b) students "achieving continuity' and seeing a piece of work through to conclusion

c) students feeling secure by knowing what is happening.

Using the 'future hypothetical" question had enabled her to raise her sights above the daily "battle" and encouraged an image of what she wanted to happen.

I took the second of the measures - students achieving continuity - and asked how Sarah usually achieved this. She described how she usually discussed with the students the purpose of each activity in order to make it explicit. As she did this she reflected that her frequent absences from class, due to her work in other classes related to a whole school project, meant this was not happening as frequently as she wanted. To compensate the class for her absences, Sarah came up with the idea of visually representing her topic in a diagram showing clearly how the pieces of work connected together. This led to a series of questions such as:

"When will you do this?"

"How will you introduce this?"
"Where will the diagram be displayed?"
"How often will you refer to it ?"

By elaborating the picture in this detailed way her ideas were gradually translated into an action plan and potential difficulties could immediately be identified and addressed.

As she was talking Sarah also commented that there were too many incomplete pieces of work and half-finished classroom displays which she felt might be contributing to the students' sense of incoherence. Completing the displays would, she felt, be helpful to both the students' and her own sense of purpose. She seemed momentarily overwhelmed by the prospect of finishing all the pieces of work. We reflected back on her original goal and considered how helpful completing all the pieces of work would be in achieving this. Finally she resolved to decide which pieces were important and which could be left. By this point in the discussion, Sarah was looking visibly more relaxed, was talking more positively about her situation, probably because she now had two clear things she could try out.

Turning to the goal of achieving a sense of security for the students we re-capped on the current situation where the teacher would be out of the classroom, sometimes at short notice, and the class would be covered by colleagues. After a moment, the idea emerged of a timetable which would show who would be covering and when. Making her absences more predictable would hopefully help the students cope with them better.

This raised a related issue that the students often wanted to speak with her when she was not in the class and the teachers covering her class were finding this disruptive. We considered how the students could speak to her in her absence and the idea of letter writing emerged. As we discussed this idea she became excited by its potential, suggesting as a creative solution to the problem an interactive "post-box" by which she and the students could correspond.

It was interesting that Sarah no longer felt the need to discuss the first of the issues raised concerning students staying on task, as she judged that this issue would resolve itself. Erickson (quoted in Rossi, 1980) stated that "therapy is often a matter of tipping the first domino". However, she was still concerned about the students' perception that the disruptive behaviour of some was seen by others as going unchecked. I asked what she thought, from the students' point of view, needed to be done. She paused, smiled and considered the possibility of asking them directly. In this way she might be able to establish what the students' goals were. Finally, and following on from this, we felt it would be important to give the students clear feedback about times when they were helpful and co-operative, the idea being to encourage more of the desired behaviour.

In the very short space of half an hour the teacher had identified goals for change and set about planning to achieve them. She was able to draw on a fund of interesting ideas and use her knowledge of the class and her professional expertise to develop these. Using de Shazer's (1988) coding of a client's relationship to the therapeutic context, Sarah was definitely a customer motivated to find a solution.

Three weeks later I spoke again with Sarah. Her first comment, accompanied by a wide smile, was the clear statement, "I feel much more positive now". She placed herself as 8/9 on a scale where 10 signified she had achieved everything she wanted. Sarah described how she had gone away from our previous discussion and immediately set up the "post box". The success of this strategy had surpassed her hopes and she talked with enthusiasm about how the students not only wrote to her but had also begun to use letter writing as a way of solving their own problems. They would write down a difficulty and post it in an envelope into the box. A couple of days later, when Sarah approached the student, they would often state that it was no longer a problem because they had sorted it out themselves. An interesting development of this could be to ask the student how they had managed to sort things out and thereby make explicit the successful strategies they had been using.

Sarah had tried out all the ideas, apart from the classroom displays, mentioning, with a wry smile, the huge relief she experienced when she had discussed with the students the selection of the pieces of work to be finished. At first, Sarah had viewed not completing the classroom displays as an expression of failure, as something she should have done. We then rated the interventions in terms of their usefulness and she felt that the classroom displays were probably the least useful. In this way the suggestions that Sarah took away from meetings were managed in different ways. For instance, some were directly useful, some evolved with use, others were not viable. In all of these Sarah was best placed to judge the most productive areas in which to use her energy.

So what had worked for Sarah and why?
Sarah was asked to evaluate the consultation - particularly those things she had found most useful.

Making the best use of time available
Sarah stated that she had felt a sense of relief at being able to talk to someone from outside the school for an uninterrupted period of time, adding that she had reached the stage where she felt she had to do something but was unable to move forward without sharing her concerns.

Schools are complex systems faced with the pressures of enormous legislative changes and fewer resources. Head teachers, as managers, are therefore faced with the difficult decision about where best to deploy these resources and how to make the best use of time available. Setting aside a period of time with an individual teacher can be considered a luxury, and yet half an hour used effectively can lead to an enormous saving of time in the long-term; if the teacher eventually feels confident in the classroom, it may prevent the referral of students for more detailed individual work. In addition the head teacher may be spared many hours of overseeing students in their office and discussing behaviour with them.

Who decides what should be discussed?
Sarah stated that the time had enabled her to focus on a particular problem away from other issues in the school. We believe she was thus able to talk confidently about what she wanted to discuss, rather than having a pre-conceived idea about what she felt she ought to discuss.

Implicit in this is the value of the consultee leaving a discussion feeling they have been listened to. Solution focused approaches emphasise this by advocating a "fit with the client". In this the consultant needs to be sensitive to the way information is received and questions are answered. Any indication of embarrassment or discomfort should lead to a change in the approach by the consultant. One of the most useful indicators can be the "yes, but ..." response - the presence of "but" half way through a sentence indicating that the idea, or whatever, is being rejected. de Shazer (1985) suggests that such responses inform the worker that she or he should reconsider the chosen direction.

Hope that change will occur
Sarah also commented that the discussion, in helping her focus on how she would like things to be, had given her hope. Furman and Ahola (1992) high-light the need to focus on areas which foster hope; problems might well be maintained simply by repeated talk about them, thus engendering a feeling of hopelessness.

Action verses ideas
Finally Sarah commented on the value of ideas which were immediately accessible to her and sufficiently detailed to allow the formulation of an action plan. It is also notable that the ideas were accessible because they were developed by Sarah herself.

The corridor conversation
This case study describes a consultation with a teacher in a primary school and illustrates how in a very brief discussion it may be better to clarify issues and goals as opposed to trying to give instant advice. In particular, it high-lights the importance of finding the key question which helps to tease out the pertinent issues. I had no background information beyond the first name of the pupil as this did not constitute a formal referral, and the purpose was to help the teacher plan her approach with the child.

A teacher approached me at the beginning of the break period in the staff room to ask if I could talk with her about a 5 year old pupil she was very concerned about. We had twelve minutes until she would be required to collect her class from the playground.

The teacher began with a graphic description of the pupil's disruptive behaviour which was causing serious management difficulties. She was at a loss, having tried a number of strategies, none of which had made a difference. I asked the teacher what would be a helpful way of using the time available. She stated without hesitation, "to stop Ian from kicking other students and tearing up their work". I began to explore this in more depth with questions such as:

"Have there been any times over the last couple of weeks when this behaviour has not occurred?"

"What was different about these times?"

"Have any of the strategies you have tried worked a little bit?"

This was an attempt to look at exceptions which could provide the basis of a solution. However, each time the teacher answered, she referred quickly back to a discussion about how difficult Ian's behaviour was, with further detailed examples. Although it felt as though the teacher was simply complaining about the pupil, she had voluntarily asked to discuss her concerns and clearly wanted something different to happen. In solution focused terms I had not yet found the most productive and fitting method of facilitating change.

I therefore decided to widen the discussion by asking, "What, for you, would be first sign of progress?" This proved to be the turning point of the meeting. Her reply, "Well, I would be able to talk to Ian about his behaviour", revealed a whole new area of discussion which turned out to be the source of the teacher's frustration. Her effective management strategies with other students were based on developing a strong personal relationship and negotiating alternative ways of behaving with them. With Ian she had been unable to "find a way through". She felt de-skilled and unable to influence his behaviour.

By reflecting on the situation the teacher appeared to develop a new perspective on the area of difficulty and commented that Ian seemed to find conversations with her "threatening". We were then able to explore ways of making conversations less threatening and the idea of a shared activity emerged (building with lego) during which the teacher could talk with Ian; she felt this would make the conversation more "casual". The idea was extended with the possibility of using stories or plastic characters to discuss specific behaviours. The last few minutes were spent discussing the location, the best time and how to follow up these discussions.

On subsequent visits to the school no further discussions about Ian's behaviour were needed.

Jim

In the following example a series of meetings are described (lasting approximately half an hour each) looking at the behaviour of an individual pupil. Although the pupil and parent were present at the final meeting, direct contact with them was minimal, and the significant work was in consultation with the teacher.

The first consultation took place with the teacher, Liz, during a meeting with staff when new referrals were being discussed and ongoing work briefly reviewed.

I was first told that the teachers were concerned that a boy, Jim (aged 5) was reported to be engaging in difficult behaviour, was ignoring requests from the teacher and hitting other pupils. I was also informed that following marital violence the family had a social worker and it was clearly stated that Jim hated his father. Already at this stage, however, a variation in his pattern of behaviour was noted; he was said to have been "more settled" before Christmas, and then had begun to display difficult behaviour again.

I next saw the class teacher alone and asked what strategies had been tried with Jim. The teacher immediately gave examples of several attempts at change. She noted that he was friendly in one-to-one situations. He was a little better when sitting near her and he would finish off work if sent to the head teacher because of excessively difficult behaviour; he would also stop when sent to another class.

I then asked, "What minimal changes would Jim have to make in order to become acceptable to school?" The teacher replied, "For him to be more co-operative with school". I then asked for examples of this; what she would first notice or see? Liz replied that Jim would "work with others and not interfere" and also "sit on the carpet during class activities". Immediately the teacher added that during the last two days he had done just this; an example of pre-session change (O'Hanlon and Weiner-Davis, 1989). I asked why she thought this might be so but she could not think of a reason. I next asked the teacher to carry out a series of what were essentially observation tasks. First, to make a list of 'what works' with Jim, second to "consider what is different when things work. Is there any kind of pattern or not?" The teacher was also asked to consider which specific behaviours were of most concern.

A few weeks later I met the teacher again. She had fully implemented the previous suggestions and came with a hand-written list of activities entitled "What works sometimes". Some examples were:

- If he is in a "good mood", sit him at the front, giving him physical affection and talking with him.
- When in a "bad mood", the "physical connection" works, for example, a hand on his shoulder.
- To set up a sort of "competition" with a boy who seems to act as a role model for Jim and whom he liked.
- Clear, firm instructions, telling him what is expected from him.

The focus of this second consultation was to discuss these ideas in detail, to suggest she continued with those activities which worked well and express my admiration at her work and conscientiousness.

Some time passed and I was informed that Jim was making good progress. In order to review this in more detail a meeting was held five months after the original referral. The class teacher reported significant improvements. To gauge this I asked a scaling question, suggesting 1 as Jim's worst and 10 as his perfect behaviour. She said he had started at 1, that 6 would be acceptable, and that he had sometimes been 7.

A sustained sequence of questions explored how she had achieved this. The practical ideas discussed previously were listed, plus many other comments, particularly on how "rapport" had been established, and how our discussions had given her the confidence to ignore the advice of another teacher to let him do as he liked, an idea she had not favoured.

On this visit I also looked at Jim's reading and saw his mother. Her presence suggested her support for the teacher and myself, yet she did not request any further involvement by myself, perhaps due to her extensive involvement with other workers.

Jim made enormous progress. I hope that at least the solution focused approach enabled the teacher and myself to co-operate and perhaps gave the teacher greater confidence to trust her own judgements. A year and three months later, Jim was still making good progress, and doing very well with a new teacher.

An issue of school management
During meetings with teachers, not only are individual students discussed, but almost any issue can be broached. In the following example, the head teacher sought to discuss her worries about the behaviour of a class. The head had very little time and was not seeking extended consultation, as will become apparent. In this real world situation, there was certainly no time to consider the nature of this request, whether it was 'clear' and so forth. I decided to "go with the flow" and to see if anything useful could be done. The whole exchange lasted no more than 20 minutes.

The head asked quickly whether I wouldn't mind discussing her concerns. She explained that during the last year or so, due to long term absences, the class had been covered by a number of cover or supply teachers. Not surprisingly, the general behaviour of the class had greatly deteriorated and this was creating problems in the wider school context. The pupils were now engaging in fights, damage to property, misbehaviour at lunch times in the dining hall and playground and in general "anti-social behaviour".

I asked what strategies had already been used. At first, the head, who has a good sense of humour, said "nagging". As is typical of many interviews, she did not just list her strategies, but shifted the focus back to concerns. She then mentioned another strategy: "I go on and on", and added, "but I don't know the class". She pointed out how it was difficult if you don't know a class well, yet need to go in to discuss behaviour problems. This was beginning to ruin her relationship with the class. She suggested that she needed to do "something positive".

I then continued to ask questions about what the head had found to work with this class, what was actually working at the time. She listed several things including keeping the whole class in, giving lectures, and telling individuals off in public.

My next idea was to explore either hypothetical solutions or first signs of progress. The head, however, made it very clear that she wished to focus only on the present situation as the class teacher would be returning shortly and her concern was what could be done in the interim. The discussion therefore focused on what the head teacher was going to do, and what her "decision" was to be. The following action plans were outlined:

1) Give a very serious public talk to the whole school about the situation.

2) Go into the class more for positive interactions, for example, to do drama, which the head enjoyed.

3) Think about "indirect systems of management", that is, some other method than students being sent directly to her if there were difficulties.

We finished with a brief discussion about how some students conform to a norm, be it one of disruption or quiet work. The norm for this class had evidently deteriorated and we decided that this was more a reflection of organisational chaos than that of the pupils being intrinsically difficult. (These ideas are discussed by Measor and Woods, 1984). We also discussed the various sources of "influence" a leader can have, for example, status, liking, punishment and expertise (Schmuck and Schmuck, 1971). We decided that the situation had driven the head to rely too much on punitive measures, whereas Schmuck and Schmuck suggest that positive measures are more effective.

The head thanked me and said she found this useful. What my write-up does not catch is how intense, fast, and somewhat emotional this interview was. In the middle part I really felt I had gone wrong; it perhaps illustrates how direction can be found again by standing back for a while, listening carefully, and considering alternative directions. Some time later the head said she had tackled the difficulties with new resolve and improvements had been made.

Conclusion

One of the most striking features of the solution focused approach is that it allows great flexibility. It seems to allow the rapid recognition of straightforward situations, and provides suggestions for moving forward in more complex consultations. Many teachers who ask for a consultation have already thought hard and long about the problem. Many have a great deal of experience and will already be trying out particular strategies; the situation may be very difficult, but they are coping. A consultant using the solution focused approach can make full use of these strengths and resources.

A considerable amount of our work involves brief conversations. The application of solution focused thinking in this context has facilitated some very productive discussions with teachers. The type of questions and areas of focus help to stop us from being forced into an "expert" role and encourages collaboration in the search for solutions. It has provided a clear framework in which to support teachers, parents and other professionals in their work with students.

The solution focused approach makes no judgements about a person's style of management, in that it does not come with a ready-made theory of how teachers should teach, rather it helps teachers expand those aspects which work well for them. Being released from the pressure of giving "expert advice", the consultant seems to be able to engage in greater creativity of thought.

CHAPTER SIX

Classroom management and organisational change

Organisational work could be defined as attempts made at changing the actual functioning or structure of a system, e.g. a classroom or playground community. Essentially, this work does not focus on individual students or staff. One approach is organisational consultation as discussed in the last chapter. Another well-established approach is the use of in-service training where, typically, workshops are held and participants asked to try out new ideas. Other approaches could be described as more participative: the visiting workers may not only consult with staff but, as it were, begin to actually take part in certain activities of the school. For example, by attending staff meetings, talking with students, and making direct observations of everyday activities.

This chapter contains examples of organisational work using solution focused ideas. In general, the systems we have so far chosen to work with have been on a small scale, such as the classroom.

Our first attempts

Over several years the authors have carried out a number of projects in schools (Rhodes, 1987). Much of our early work was influenced by the action research model defined by Cohen and Manion (1985) as "small-scale intervention in the functioning of the real world and a close examination of the effects of such intervention". They go on to argue that action research has two basic stages: a "diagnostic" stage in which problems are analysed and hypotheses developed, and then a "therapeutic" stage in which attempts are made to try out the hypotheses in a real world situation.

Although most of our early projects met with some measure of success, several doubts began to creep in about the efficacy of this approach for the type of work we were involved in (although we had no doubt about its use in some situations, for example, in a completely new context, or for increasing the knowledge base of the consultant and consultee concerning a particular kind of situation). Two questions of particular concern were:

a) Is this the best use of the time available? Collecting data using activities such as observations or interviews is very time-consuming, as is the analysis of the data.

b) What are the links between the data collected and the strategies finally discussed at the planning meeting?

Several years ago, before using solution focused ideas, both authors were involved in a large scale project aimed at changing the level of disruption in a school playground. A vast amount of data was collected through observations and interviews. The actual practical ideas were developed by a series of joint planning meetings involving representatives of the staff and the two psychologists. The practical ideas had, it seemed to us, no clear and straight-forward link with the data when the project was finished. de Shazer (1985) refers to this when he describes the discontinuity between problem and solution patterns; namely, that ideas found out about a problem pattern were not used in the design of an intervention towards a solution.

There are many possible explanations here; perhaps we collected the wrong data, or perhaps we just weren't inventive enough in analysing the data. However, from a solution focused perspective, it may well be that such extensive data collection was not really necessary at all, and that we could have begun the creative construction of new ideas with staff much sooner by simply asking them what they wanted to change and then building on these ideas. Watzlawick et al (1974) give many examples of situations where a plan of action is determined by creative solution finding rather than analysing the problem. They tell how during riots in Paris in the seventeenth century a commander is asked to clear a square of the 'rabble' by ordering his men to open fire. Before the command is given he addresses the crowd. "I have been ordered to shoot at the rabble. However, I can see before me a number of respectable citizens. Therefore, I would like them to leave first before my men start shooting the rabble." The square cleared in seconds!

The work described in this chapter can be seen as some of our first attempts to investigate the following questions, namely, in what ways can organisational work be carried out a) without elaborate collection of data, and b) without necessarily forming a clear hypothesis of why or how there comes to be a problem? We were, of course, also interested in how the use of the solution focused questions might be experienced by participants. For example, do people seem encouraged by their use?

The next step was to design the outline of a solution focused project. Variations of this outline have now been used in several projects, as yet very tentatively. Our work to date suggests the value of adapting the number of steps from project to project.

Stage 1 pre-session change

What could be done in the very first stages of a project? In solution focused work clients are often asked to notice any changes between making an appointment and the first session. We adapted this idea and used a questionnaire approach to encourage pre-session preparation. Sometimes just thinking about a situation may facilitate a new way of viewing it which, in turn, may lead to different approaches. The first two questions required the teacher to reflect on the current situation, the following three questions looked at exceptions and goals.

1. What are the main difficulties with the class?
(Please try to give examples.)
Although this is looking at the problem we felt it would be useful to reflect specifically on this as a first step to looking at areas to change. It is also possible that teachers will expect us to want to know about their concerns and why it is they are requesting a project.

2. Why do you think this class is difficult?
There may be a number of explanations about the nature of the difficulties. What will be most important is the beliefs of the particular teacher(s) involved.

3. When, and in what situations, is this class better?
This begins the search for exceptions.

4. What strategies have tended to work with this class?
This draws on the strengths and teaching style of the teacher.

5. Are there any strategies you wish to try out and what are they?
Are there any ready formed ideas or thoughts which could be developed?

Stage 2 Planning meeting
This has have four distinct phases:

1. Sorting out the "technical" details
This involves details such as the number and duration of meetings, who should be involved, who needs to know about what is happening and what they would need to know.

The importance of this stage has become more and more apparent as we have progressed in our work. The suggestions from David Campbell, et al, (1989) have been particularly useful in aiding understanding. They define the process as the "entry conditions", emphasising the need to establish a clear contract between all the parties involved to clarify roles and expectations. It is their experience that the success of a piece of work could depend on the structure established at this stage. Our experience tends to bear this out.

2. Goal Setting
The next step is to establish the criteria for a successful outcome, in the belief that the clearer these are the easier it will be to know how to work towards them. de Shazer (1985) states that one of the most common reasons for failure is a poorly defined goal which when achieved doesn't make a difference.

Examples of questions include:
"What would you like to take away from this project that would make you feel it had been worthwhile?"

"How will you know when the project is complete?"
"What will be the first sign of progress?"
"Imagine it is a month's time and the situation is how you would like it to be. What is happening?"
"What else? What else?"

3. The search for exceptions

Are there any times when the desired situation is happening? This can be explored with questions such as:

"What improvements have you noticed?"
"How could you explain these?"
"What are you doing differently?"
"What is happening at these times that is different?"
"What might someone else notice?"
"How might you get it to happen again?"

Again, the situations are explored in detail to establish a clear and tangible picture.

4. Setting Tasks.

These can vary depending on the information gained. Using the structure of the formula tasks described by de Shazer (1985) the options can be as follows:

- If it is working well, carry on doing it. Sometimes simply the reassurance that an idea is a good one is all that's needed.

- Observation tasks - try and note down times when things are a little better and observe what is happening that is different at these times - who is doing what.

- Experiment with different approaches and see which ones or which bits of these approaches are the most useful. The emphasis on aspects or details is important. It can be easy to dismiss something completely if it does not seem to be working and yet the essence of the idea may be fine.

- Try something different. This is left deliberately vague in the belief that a different response to a situation can, whatever it is, change the interacting patterns.

Stage 3 Review meeting
This involves several parts.

1. An activity involving direct contact with the system
This has most commonly been direct observation, though this is not the only possibility and one encourages flexibility in pursuing whatever is felt to be appropriate. In general, the aim of our observations has been to look for strengths. Another frequently used activity has been to interview pupils. For example, about their interests or how they experience the class.

2. Discussion about what has been tried and what is going well
Again we hope to encourage as clear a picture as possible with questions such as:
> "What will other people have noticed about what you are doing differently?"
> "What was it about this particular approach that you think works well for you?"
> "What does this show you about yourself?"
> "If you had to advise someone in a similar situation what would you tell them?"

Expansion questions can be used to explore a particular point:
> "Who would be the first to notice?"
> "What would they notice?"
> "How would you explain this difference?"

3. Goals, tasks, and further compliments
Goals are essential and need to be reconsidered at all stages. Specific questions can be asked at this meeting, such as:
> "Are your goals still the same?"
> "What would the next step be?"
> "Are there any other areas you would like to consider?"

If the previous task has been to continue something which was already working, then it can be useful to verify whether this is still the case. For previously agreed observation tasks, it can be illuminating to discuss what has been recorded. The latter might well contain vital new information. Compliments, can of course focus on what has just been observed. In our experience, these comments are very much valued by the teacher. It would seem that compliments of any kind are sometimes a rare commodity in schools.

Stage 4 Final meeting
This essentially involves a repeat of the previous stage. The important thing is to check out at the beginning of the meeting what would need to happen for the participants to know that it had been useful.

Putting it into practice

The first two accounts in this chapter look at the application of this structure in two projects, both of which focus on the middle area of organisational development, i.e. the classroom. The first account is given by a colleague, Fiona Norman, an educational psychologist who also works in Hackney, about a piece of work she carried out while on a regular contract visit to a primary school.

Project A: "Music is my love and inspiration"

Negotiating the project
The head teacher and class teacher discussed their concerns about a difficult class which had experienced considerable disruption and lack of continuity over the past two years. Particular concern about six students was also high-lighted. It was agreed that the current class teacher should continue to have the class for the next academic year and that the most effective use of my time as educational psychologist for the school, would be to work with the class as a whole, as many of the issues affected the whole class. I was able to offer three sessions of one and a half hours over the next two terms. I discussed with both the head teacher and the class teacher their expectations of the project to ensure a shared understanding of what the project might involve, including the expec-

tations of my role. They were both interested in exploring different ways of working and new ideas, with the aim of increasing the achievement of the students in the class.

First project meeting

In the first meeting the teacher high-lighted her concern that the three ability groups in her class were underachieving. When asked to consider what she would like to happen differently the teacher commented, "To improve the quality of achievement in the class and for the students to be more excited and motivated in their work". We then focused on what was working well rather than pursuing in more detail the teacher's concerns, thus influencing the direction of discussion into "solution talk". In response to the question "What progress have you noticed in the students?", the class teacher identified a number of recent improvements, for example, the students were beginning to do more creative writing using proper punctuation and re-drafting. Additionally, reading levels were up and more complex problem solving was being tackled. In asking how the class teacher had achieved this, the intention was to high-light the strategies she was already using and to emphasise that she had already found some ways of encouraging the students in their achievement.

Towards the end of the session I asked the teacher about her strengths and interests. Because she initially found this difficult (maybe because it is a rarely asked question!), it was important to keep asking "And what else? And what else?" Eventually she spoke animatedly about her love of music and poetry ("music is my love and inspiration"). She also mentioned that she had not been able to use the things she enjoyed in teaching with this class because she had expended so much energy managing the difficult behaviour.

End of the session

Towards the end of the session, after a short break, I complimented the teacher on her many qualities, strengths and skills. I also indicated I might write any further thoughts in a letter as I felt I needed more time to think about what had been discussed. The teacher in turn asked if I would observe the class on my next visit.

Reflections
Reflecting on the session afterwards I felt that the goals had not been clear enough and that exploring the teacher's strengths and interests would have been more useful nearer the beginning of the session as this provided a rich source of information. I also thought of other questions, and included these in a letter of which the following is an extract:

"One thing that came across to me was your modesty about the skills you bring to teaching. In particular you mentioned music as being your love and inspiration and that you love poetry. I wish I had asked you more about this, especially as it is clear it is important to you and you have not been able to use these to their best with this class. I was wondering what would need to happen for you to be able to use these strengths with the class and how this might link with the quality of their learning, achievement and excitement. I would be interested to hear your thoughts about this when we next meet."

I also asked the teacher to notice any changes in the classroom and to think further about what would make the classroom observation worthwhile.

Peer consultation
Between sessions I asked a colleague for a consultation. This was valuable in helping me to formulate ways of eliciting tangible goals. At this point I was concerned about the elusive nature of the teacher's concerns, i.e. "quality of achievement and excitement in learning". The discussion helped the formulation of some questions:

"What would I see if I came into your classroom that would be different?"

"What would other people, e.g. the head teacher, other teachers, parents, see?"

It was also helpful to remember the importance of focusing on small
steps:
"What are the minimum changes that would be acceptable?"
"What would be the first signs that these changes had occurred?"

We also decided to explore past successes, because the teacher, although
currently faced with a difficult class, was competent and experienced.
To be reminded of this competency may in itself effect change.

Session two
Three weeks later I met with the teacher again. She had decided to
introduce poetry to the class and wanted me to observe the first half of
the lesson. The head teacher would release her for the second half so
we could discuss the next stages in the project.

I asked the teacher what would make it a useful observation for her.
She high-lighted the following areas for me to focus on: the motivation
of the students and their response to her teaching style, her teaching
style itself and the quality of her interaction with the students.

During the lesson I talked to a number of students about their views
of the lessons. This proved to be a fruitful source of ideas. Several students who told me they hated poetry and that the lesson was boring,
went on to reveal how they enjoyed funny poems and already had a
repertoire of poets they knew. In particular the students had shown a
negative response to a worksheet presented on a traditional poem and
a dictionary exercise to find the meanings of words used. In contrast the
students were most motivated when asked for their own views and had
the opportunity to write their own poems. I also noted that the students
were able to work well in pairs.

To the teacher, I pointed out that she stated clearly what she wanted from the students, modelled what they had to do and engaged with
their ideas. I had also observed the teacher was able to anticipate when
the students were getting stuck.

This information provided a useful basis on which to decide how the
project could proceed. It gave an indication of the type of
activity/approach which the students enjoyed and perhaps reassured the

teacher that poetry could be a source of motivation for this class. The teacher was now clear she would like to develop a class topic on poetry as she felt this would be the best way to encourage achievement and motivation in their learning. Minimally she wanted the students to be "more confident and to enjoy their work". Having established a clear direction for change it was easier now to clarify specific steps and develop them into workable actions.

I asked the teacher to imagine what I would see if I came into her classroom in six weeks time that would tell me she had achieved what she wanted. She replied that all the students would produce one piece of poetry for a wall display and that they would read out their poetry in a class assembly. They would also produce a poetry book for the head teacher to use in future assemblies.

A time scale of five weeks was felt to be realistic and the teacher rated herself as a 7 on a confidence scale that she would be able to achieve all of this. Although this was a high rating, I asked what would increase the rating. This opened out a very interesting discussion about the need to create a balance between planning/getting things clear in her mind and giving the students scope. The teacher usually achieved this balance in areas outside of the National Curriculum pressures, such as art and craft with which she felt more able to follow the student's lead. It seemed in this situation she could be more relaxed and confident about the student's capabilities.

I suggested that maybe for the duration of the project she could imagine poetry as a craft activity and could experiment with balancing her planning and letting the student's have some scope. This would give her the opportunity to notice times when she felt comfortable with the balance and what seemed to suit the students best.

As the teacher had talked a lot about having high standards for herself and the students I asked, in terms of the project, "What would be the icing on the cake?" Her answer: that one or two students would produce something that would surprise her.

Final session

Six weeks later I was told by the class teacher that she couldn't stop the students writing poetry, they were all writing poems and had really surprised her with some of their work - at which point she produced a folder. The teacher was clearly pleased by the results of the project. Thinking about the balance of planning had changed her perceptions in such a way that she felt she could trust herself to follow the ideas and interests of the students. In doing so the teacher felt she had been able to think about the student's contributions to their learning and develop these through the achievable goals.

Conclusion

This was a first experiment in applying solution focused thinking to a class project. At times, I was unsure in which direction we were heading. However, the progressive construction of clear goals also seemed to play a key role in helping the teacher to fully deploy all her talents and achieve the excitement and motivation which had seemed so hard to define.

Project B: So many ideas, so much to do

The initial discussion with the head teacher revealed her concern about the level of disruptive behaviour and poor standard of work in a particular class. The class, having been taught by a succession of supply teachers, was now being co-taught by two teachers for part of the week each. Both these teachers were experienced and had taught in the school for a while. The two teachers had met prior to taking over the class, had negotiated working on separate projects and they had regular meetings to discuss what they were doing. The head teacher felt they would appreciate the opportunity to discuss some specific strategies and approaches to help settle the class.

Setting the scene - first planning meeting

The teachers were keen to talk about the class and came up with a large number of areas they wanted to look at - an almost overwhelming number. The first task was therefore to refine these down into a smaller, more manageable number; either those of most concern or those most amenable to change. Apart from the difficulty of co-ordinating many different strands of thought, there would simply not be the time to explore so many areas in sufficient detail.

Four goals, things that would be happening in the class if the difficulties were solved, were chosen:

a. The students would be working on task.

b. The teachers would be calm in difficult or provoking situations.

c. The students would have strategies they could use themselves in difficult situations.

d. The students would be working co-operatively.

As we talked, a number of exceptions and successful strategies emerged. For example, the class was better in the mornings than the afternoons, and afternoon registration was high-lighted as a particularly unpleasant time. Reflecting on this, one of the teachers commented that it might be better to leave the registration for ten minutes and then call it.

The teachers also described a number of successful strategies they had already used, including, being firm and following through instructions, having clear sanctions and compiling lists of what was going well with the class. Almost as an afterthought one teacher commented that the class had actually been better than she had thought. When asked in what way, she described how their improved behaviour had been noticed around the school. This was an important point for the teachers, that they were seeming to have an effect on the class and that this effect had been noticed.

The session ended with a task to observe what else was working well in each of the four areas identified. We hoped this would help to continue the direction of solution innovation and it was also possible that important areas of exceptions had not yet been revealed. As an extension of this a letter was sent asking each of the teachers to complete a scaling question relating to the four areas - comparing where the class had been when they first took over and where they were now. Any improvements could be explored, if the class were the same we could look at what had been done to keep the class at that level, and specific areas needing more consideration could be high-lighted.

Session two

During the second session the rating scales and what was working well in each of the four areas the teachers had identified were explored. For example, we asked the teachers how they would explain the improvements, exactly what they were doing, what the student's response had been and what other examples they could think of.

a. Keeping on task

	Teacher A	Teacher B
Where the class had been:	2/3	4
Where they had moved to:	5	6

The teachers were able to identify a number of strategies which promoted the desired behaviour of the students working. These included organising short structured activities (the teachers felt that the key elements of this structure included a clear definition of what was expected), examples the students could use as a guide and clear feedback about what they were doing. The students settled most quickly to tasks they perceived as exciting and worked well in pairs where they could support each other if experiencing difficulties.

b. Being calm.

	Teacher A	Teacher B
Where the class had been:	2/3	4
Where they had moved to:	5	6

The teachers had both observed that when they themselves were calm, the class were also a lot calmer. They both agreed they felt calmer in situations where they were clear about what to do (i.e. through a prior discussion or an established rule) which helped them to approach the situation with more confidence. A list was then compiled of the most useful of these:

- don't punish the whole class, only those who have been difficult
- give a warning
- telling the students what will be looked for in terms of good behaviour
- working out a reward system, e.g. earning an extra ten minutes play for calm behaviour during the last five minutes of the day, helping in the nursery for individual students

All these ideas were very simple - the value was in ordering them in a structured way so they were easily accessible to the teachers.

c. Dealing with conflict.

	Teacher A	Teacher B
Where the class had been:	1/2	4
Where they had moved to:	4	5

The teachers had already used a cartoon to discuss with the class how they responded to difficult situations. Almost without exception the student's response had been, "Get an adult". Although a useful strategy, the teachers were keen to look at ways of getting the students to help themselves. A number of ideas emerged:
- making time to discuss situations with students - this followed on from a comment made by one of the teachers; "If I actually listen to them they seem to have more confidence"
- developing close links with parents
- establishing a consistent structure for the removal of privileges

At this stage time ran out. Although it was not possible to look at the last area, i.e. students working co-operatively, the teachers felt that success in the other areas would have a bearing on this. The session ended with compliments from us about the teachers' level of thought and positive approach.

Although another meeting was scheduled, the teachers subsequently informed us that they did not feel any further meetings were necessary. This was not to say all the problems had "disappeared" but rather enough had changed for the teachers to feel confident they could continue without outside assistance.

In-service training

A further area of development which arose recently was that of in-service training (INSET). This is an important area of work which can take many different forms.

A request was made by a nursery school for some input on the topics of self-esteem and motivation. This type of work can be very rewarding but can equally prove to be very difficult. One of the key issues is to establish with the staff the information and ideas they are most interested in. This sounds logical and simple; in reality it can be very difficult. One of the authors can recall a situation several years ago where members of staff were asked individually if they would be interested in a piece of work. It was only when they were together as a group that dissension was evident and arguments actually broke out. The session was possibly useful as a discussion for the staff but it certainly scuppered any productive INSET.

Remembering the importance of negotiating work at the early stages (Campbell, et al, 1989), it was decided to use some of the questions derived from solution focused thinking to help establish exactly what would be helpful for this particular school. At a meeting with the head teacher the following questions were asked:

"How will you know if the INSET has been successful?"

"How will you know whether the children have higher self esteem and are more motivated?"

"What questions would you like answered?"

"What methods/approaches are you already using that work well?"

The head teacher agreed to consult with the staff and sent some information. Judging by the thoughtfulness of the information sent by the school the staff were clearly very motivated and the initial questions had seemed to facilitate their thinking.

What we do that already works

We talk to the children and show interest in them

We praise children on an individual basis

We talk about children who are absent so they know that if they are away they will always be missed

We have photos of the children around the nursery

We talk to parents about working with their children at home

We display the children's work

We do an activity ourselves and invite children to join the activity

How competent are we already?

For 90% of the children 7 out of 10, for the other 10%, 3 out of 10.

How do we know when a child has good self-esteem/is well motivated?

The child:

- is happy and confident
- will produce a constant stream of quality work
- will be able to independently select activities and carry them out
- chooses appropriate friends
- plays cops and robbers without arguing

What questions do we want answered by the trainers?

What can we do with the 10%?

What can we do if we think home circumstances are to blame?

Some have high self-esteem and low motivation, others vice versa - they don't always seem to go together. What are the differences between self- esteem and motivation?

In addition, each member of staff undertook a detailed observation on an individual child, looking at how the child interacted with the other children and adults and thinking about why they had chosen the child and what it was they would like them to do differently. All this information was enormously helpful in the planning stages. With any topic there is a vast amount of information which can be used. The clarity gained about what would be useful facilitated a sifting through and a focus on what was relevant. After the INSET the head teacher commented that one of its most valuable aspects was the thinking the staff did beforehand. It had helped them to clarify their thoughts, be clear about what they were already doing and to really look closely at the children.

An advantage for the consultants was that they felt more confident about the material they were presenting and because of this the session was more relaxed. The solution focused questions also proved very useful when considering an issue raised by the group about how to involve parents positively in looking at the self-esteem of their child. There were only five minutes left of the INSET time before the lunch-break. A scaling question was used looking at where they placed themselves now, how they got there and what would need to happen to move to the next step. An exception immediately emerged about a parent with whom the nursery staff felt they had developed a very good relationship. The staff were asked what had happened to improve this relationship and if there was anything helpful they could use again. The session ended without any of these questions being fully answered, but importantly the staff felt they had enough to think about to be able to continue the discussion independently. This is the value of such questions; the pressure on the consultant to find an answer is pushed to one side, leaving space and confidence for people to solve their own difficulties.

Solution focused thinking and peer support
This final piece of work was carried out by a group of educational psychologists working in the London Borough of Southwark and the following account was written by two members of the team, David Keaton and Jo Talbot. It is different from the other pieces of work in that the team was working on aspects of its own functioning rather than working with other institutions.

Introduction
During a discussion about sources of stress with all the educational psychologists in our local educational authority team, a list of 'problems' was generated which was overwhelming, specifying issues about workload, office organisation and group/individual supervision, to name but three. By using a solution focused framework to concentrate on where we wanted to get to, a translation of these "problems" into solutions was

able to occur. A shift in focus towards projections of future change also enabled us to support one another at a time of particular need, due to changes in local authority support for special educational needs and covering for absent colleagues. In addition to the pressures of heavy workloads, we had recently experienced the death of our inspirational principal psychologist.

Context
The previous monthly meetings of our seven-person "south" team had addressed networking with other professionals and had provided a forum for mutual support. The group was led by the deputy principal educational psychologist, our line manager, who also provided individual supervision and support from which we had all benefited. When she took maternity leave our first meeting as a group without her focused our minds on the need for support at a time when our personal workloads seemed to be getting out of control. Thereafter, we met on four occasions over a period of six months; three of these meetings included the use of solution focused techniques.

Process
The use of solution focused techniques arose spontaneously when we began to discuss impossible workloads. The starting point arising out of an exchange between two members of the team, was "Why don't we use the miracle question?" Thus, the following question was put to the group and answered individually, "Imagine waking up in the morning and a miracle has happened overnight; all your stresses at work have disappeared. How would you know? What would be different?"

In responding to the miracle question, each individual generated a list of goals which were related not only to work output and the opportunities to do other things, (for example, interesting project work on behaviour management), but also to how we would feel. By diving in at the deep end we constructed a very clear picture of what a problem-free situation would look like.

At our second meeting six weeks later, we asked what had changed since the initial meeting. After noting as individuals any positive signs of change, e.g. feeling more hopeful or more in control, we considered what we had done to bring about the changes. Each member was also encouraged to consider what it was about them as individuals which had enabled this to occur, thus locating and emphasising skills, strengths and resources.

At the second meeting we also used scaling questions. Each psychologist rated on a scale of 1 to 10 (where 1 equals very stressed):
- where their current level was
- where they would want to be
- what would tell them they had achieved their target

As well as establishing individual goals this opened up a discussion about how we had moved to our current position on the scale. Again we could share what we had done that had worked. Most psychologists rated their current levels of stress at a 3 or a 4 and aimed to reach 7 or 8 by the next term. However, a confidence scaling question, "How confident are you that you will achieve this?", revealed that most psychologists felt they were unlikely to reach their desired goal. As a way of tackling this and increasing our confidence we agreed to share ideas about how to draw up individual work plans at the next meeting. The purpose was to provide a structure within which targets would be expressed in clear performance terms and set within realistic time frames. For example, having no more than five outstanding reports at any one time.

At the final session we reflected that the solution focused framework had facilitated the sharing of strategies, had reduced stress and provided a clear structure within which we could think creatively about what we would like to change. The scaling questions had helped to identify goals and also some of the factors which were preventing us from achieving them. Although we were unable to change external pressures such as the new legislation about the time taken to complete assessments, we were able to think about how to prioritise the work we had to complete and outline what we could reasonably expect ourselves to fit into the time available. Of particular importance was the focus on clear signs of progress which could be easily measured. For example: "I would only have one reminder note in my diary", "I would return to the office for at least thirty minutes each lunch-time to break up a day of appointments".

Evaluation

As a group we have always worked well together and share many common goals. Feelings of mutual trust in these sessions enabled us to drop the "I am coping" mantle. Members of the group have expressed a feeling of optimism and want to continue using the structure. Individuals have also applied the techniques used in these sessions to other areas of work in schools. An important element of this group process has been the location of personal resources and building on these strengths. A possible extension could be to use this framework within the supervision and appraisal system that the service will be developing over the next six months.

Conclusions

In this chapter we have presented our thinking to date about methods of carrying out project work. It is probably true to say that although project work is exciting it is also the most difficult area of our work, partly due to the fact that schools are complex social systems which defy precise description and understanding. An attempt to try and work out a map of a secondary school by one of the authors in order to determine the groupings and interrelationships, power structures, etc., quickly demonstrated that the map varied according to who was being asked. It would seem that in any social reality people have multiple, sometimes contradictory, perspectives; this is one reason why such work is so challenging.

However, a number of key researches have shown that the same kinds of pupils will be different in different schools, i.e. that effective schools can make a positive difference to the behaviour and academic progress of students, (for example, Rutter, et al 1979), and hence attention to this area has potentially great benefits. The notion of looking at school systems has received a lot of attention over the past two decades and educational psychologists in particular were influenced by writers such as Burden (Gillham, 1978) who advocated systems work with its focus on social context as an important area of development. The interest for educational psychologists and teachers is the potential for considering primary prevention (Caplan, 1970) as opposed to just secondary or tertiary intervention; that is, by looking at aspects of schools such as the structures, procedures and ethos it is possible to encourage the desired behaviour as opposed to dealing with the consequences of undesired behaviour.

A number of different and successful ways of carrying out systems work have been developed using diverse conceptual frameworks; Frederickson (Jones and Frederickson, 1990) discusses several of these. Many types of work are referred to as "systems work", although Frederickson makes the point that for something to be called systems work it should be defined or informed by systems theory. We generally believe that solution focused work is informed by a systems perspective but as we are not making any particular claim that it does so, we have adopted the more neutral term "organisational work" in this book.

The intention is not to look in detail at these other methods but to make some general points about the application of a solution focused framework to this area of work and some of the things we have found most useful. In doing so, reference will, however, be made to some useful literature.

1. The focus on goals at the beginning of a project clarifies potential confusion and makes good use of time available. It is all too easy to meander at the start of a project. Developing clear goals seems to encourage motivation for those involved.

2. The approach is very practical in that it encourages a focus on what works well for a particular teacher in a particular situation. Thus the solutions are tailor-made and more immediately accessible.

3. The teachers themselves are integrally involved in the formulation of the strategies. Deci and Ryan (1985) discuss research which suggests that people who are expected to carry out decisions need to be involved in the process of making them. This leads to greater creativity and commitment.

4. Recently it has been suggested that consultants need to move away from the 'expert' role of giving "technical" advice towards a more facilitating role. Fox and Sigston (Wolfendale, et al, 1992) analyse a number of approaches an educational psychologist can use in their work with schools, using, as one of their dimensions for classifying approaches, the degree to which the expert stance is maintained. The emphasis of the

solution focused approach is very much to facilitate rather than to impose. What is appealing is the respect and validation it gives to people's ideas where the solutions are so clearly based on what they are doing or would like to try.

5. The solution focused approach to project work would seem to include all the elements high-lighted by Georgiades and Phillimore (1975) who point out various pitfalls for the systems neophyte. They high-light the need to work from a clear structure and sound methodological base. These elements include:

- the ability to listen
- working with the key people who want to change
- looking to the healthy parts of the system

6. Most project work is difficult because it can involve conflict between different people within the system. Thus, there may be many skills which people are not able to mobilise because of the difficult social atmosphere. Solution focused thinking can help to reduce conflict by its focus on solutions, collective goals and the strengths of individuals concerned.

All the work carried out so far has been small scale, namely work at the level of the classroom, and with small groups of staff. We would be interested in its application to larger systems (for example, developing whole school policies). It might well be that for large scale projects a combination will be needed with one or more of the better known approaches, for example, with soft systems methodology (Checkland, 1981, Frederickson, 1990); a particular strength of the latter method being that it helps participants to build what is termed a 'richer picture' of their social realities. This could be useful in situations of change, conflict and confusion. Another fruitful combination might be with systemic consultation (Campbell, et al, 1989) as this approach has significant things to say about the difficult aspect of starting well.

Our work is often about the individual and their immediate social group. Organisational work looks at the individual within the larger social system. The approach gives the clear message that the fault does not lie within the individual but involves an interaction of all the diverse elements. This work is difficult but if successful can have a powerful effect on many individuals.

CHAPTER SEVEN

First steps

Introduction

On a scale of 1 to 10 where 1 is a beginner at solution focused thinking and 10 is as good as you would like to be, where are you now?
- What have you done that makes you confident you have reached that point?
- How will you know you have moved onto the next point of the scale?
- How confident are you that you will improve?
- What would increase your confidence?

We made some important discoveries in our early attempts about how someone might begin to apply solution focused ideas, how teachers and students have evaluated them and made some observations on difficulties which can arise. Following on from this, certain theoretical implications and questions will be considered; in particular, how this way of thinking relates to the problem solving model and other perspectives in applied psychology. We hope some of the ideas in this chapter can help with the thoughts you may have had in considering the above questions.

Practical issues

Guidelines for beginning to work in a Solution Focused way

This section outlines some of the things we have found most useful in our first attempts. As with any new skill or approach, there is an understandable anxiety about using something you don't feel quite confident with. For some people their approach is to practice until they feel ready to unleash their new found talents on the unsuspecting world. For others they prefer to try bits out and gradually build up a store of confidence (O'Hanlon and Weiner-Davies, 1989). Whatever your particular style, there may be one or two things from the following list you find useful.

a. Plan beforehand
This is not always effective when you are dealing with people because they have the habit of thwarting even the best laid plans by introducing something completely new, or by changing the specific area of concern. However, thinking of a few key questions beforehand can at least give you an initial focus which will see you through those first few minutes of uncertainty. The whole art of conducting a creative session may lie in striking a balance between following a specific plan, and yet being flexible and aware of possible new routes to explore.

One of the authors was recently asked to see two people at short notice for a second session, due to illness of the original therapist. The two people in question asked to see someone unknown rather than wait for another appointment. A colleague (Evan George - Brief Therapy Practice), helped by suggesting the following two questions to start and finish the session:
> "If 'H' was here today, what would you be telling him about the things you have been doing since the last session?"
> "What would you like me to tell 'H' about the things we have talked about today?"

Having this "structure" in mind certainly helped the author to feel more confident and because of this she was then able to use familiar skills. My colleague was inventive at short notice. More usually we would sit down for a few moments and plan an outline of the questions we might ask. Often our plans have been nothing more elaborate than a few words; for example, stating "check out goals again" or "don't forget to ask about other people's point of view".

b. Aim for a sequence of questions
The temptation is to use bits here and there. This is fine, but doesn't give the feeling of using the whole approach. Individual questions used on their own can quickly become washed out by the problem-led story.

However, when using the whole approach the interview gathers a momentum, ideas can be explored in depth and sequences of ideas (i.e. questions shaped by the client's answers) can be developed; this is where true creativity starts.

c. Persist in a gentle way
The dialogue between consultant and consultee can have many ups and downs. Sometimes there is progress towards solutions but then the client may feel upset, hopeless, or wish to discuss new problems. Our advice is to persist gently in moving toward solution talk, while at the same time fully listening to the client. In our view, once a problem has been expressed, most clients do wish to move on to practical ideas, and do not wish to go deeper and deeper into the problem zone.

d. Be simple
A whole session or series of sessions can focus on exceptions. The temptation is sometimes to feel the need to use all the techniques all at once and maybe in the process move on too quickly. In contrast to this we would recommend proceeding at a gentle pace. We have heard of sessions where the whole time was spent on the first five minutes of waking after the miracle has happened.

e. Don't be afraid to mention the problem
The work does not become non solution focused because the problem is mentioned. Listen carefully and use the information given to move forwards. In a session observed by one of the authors, a woman was giving a long and very detailed account about everything that was wrong with her partner. It was very difficult to see any way to talk about solutions. The therapist, however, waited until the woman mentioned in passing about having to fix a door frame which was dangerous, at which point the therapist asked, "How come you know so much about woodwork?" The woman's whole manner altered as this theme was developed: a point of contact had been made.

f. Don't try to hide dilemmas

It is sometimes difficult to know which question to ask next. If in doubt, try asking the person which of two possible questions would be most helpful to them. This emphasises the co-operative nature of the work.

g. Don't be afraid to move the discussion on

Sometimes people can become voracious information givers about a particular situation. We have found the following useful in moving the discussion on to new areas:

"This is obviously very important … what information, in addition to what you have already told us, do you think would be useful in helping us solve this difficulty?"

" We have only got ten minutes left, how do you think we can best use the time to help us think about … whatever the goal is?"

Asking for permission to "interrupt" at the beginning of a meeting with many participants can also be useful.

h. Take extra breaks if you feel stuck

If a few minutes away can help you to focus on a useful area to explore then the time used will have been well employed. Some educational psychologists have expressed doubts about taking breaks; but in our experience they work very well. One approach is to say, "I would like to spend just a few minutes re-reading the notes I've taken, and thinking whether there are any further questions I'd like to ask. Would you also like to think if there are any questions you would like to ask me or anything further you would like me to know about?"

i. You do not need to invent elaborate tasks

If in doubt use compliments and maybe ask the client to think about the areas of their life they would like to have continue. Our most typical suggestion has been to continue with what is working well.

j. Use all your skills

If basic solution focus doesn't work, try something different. Using this approach does not automatically negate the other skills you have developed. We have certainly used contracts (Gurney in Scherer, ed., 1990) and other behavioural methods. We have also returned to the problem when an apparent impasse has been reached and we have felt the need for more information.

k. Reluctant clients

The reluctant client is someone who has been told to see you without being given a real choice (examples could include students at school, clients ordered by the court). This is not an easy area and needs to be handled sensitively. There are no hard and fast rules, but perhaps a useful starting point could be respecting the person's difficult position. de Shazer and Berg at a conference on this topic (1991) suggested that a question of the following kind could be asked:

" What would need to happen for the ... (head of year, etc.) to feel reassured you do not need to come and see me any more?"

Kral (1987) also suggests the possibility of asking whether the person believes they have received fair treatment. One of the authors found this extremely useful with a very unhappy young student. At first he seemed to be "sulking", but after a question concerning fairness he spoke freely.

How to get going

The majority of the work described in this book has developed through close collaboration and discussion. Working jointly helped us gain in confidence particularly during the early stages when everything was so new. In our team we have used a number of different ways to support our work.

a. Form a practice group

For a period of time we worked in a group of four, meeting once a fortnight for just under an hour. The time would be used variously to discuss casework, think about projects and perhaps most importantly to "practice" with each other. This gave us the opportunity to try out different types of questions and also feedback on what we as the "client" found useful.

b. Work jointly
There is something very reassuring about knowing someone else is there to help you with your thinking. It is also enormously helpful when reflecting on the session afterwards. None of the people we worked with objected and several commented on how helpful it was to have the views of two people.

c. Peer consultation
It is enormously helpful to be able to talk about your work with someone. It provides a focus for thinking about what has been done and makes it clearer about what the next steps could be. One of the authors has recently been involved in several discussions with a colleague about some counselling work using solution focused ideas. Although this person had attended a training course she had not felt confident about using the approach. As a result of the consultations she is now beginning to put her skills to use. As in peer tutoring (see chapter four), there may also be gains for the consultant - there is nothing like having to explain something to someone for helping one's own understanding.

What do people think?
We asked people what they thought about the work we had been doing, using the combination of a structured interview and a questionnaire including questions such as:
"What aspects of our work did you find most useful?"
"If change was achieved, how would you explain this?"
"What advice would you give someone in a similar situation?"
"What will your next step be?"

When considering the answers we received, a number of themes emerged.

a. Rebuilding morale
This seems to rekindle a hope that change can occur. Frank (1986) speculates that the main difference between people who seek therapy, and those who don't, is that the former have lost hope and have

become demoralised. It seems that many of the people we worked with needed to rebuild their confidence and find some belief that things could improve. And furthermore, that it was within their power to make this happen:

"Once I could imagine what things could be like ... it gave me hope."

"Don't give up."

"Steven now knows he can learn."

"When we began to work, I can remember feeling as though I was failing with him."

b. It respects autonomy

We hope the many examples in this book have shown a respect for the autonomy of those we have worked with. This quality is hard to define, yet seems to be ingrained in the very nature of the questions asked. The following quotes suggest that autonomy was an important factor:

"You have to do things yourself. Other people can help but it's up to you."

"The most useful aspect of the work was helping James find ways of helping himself."

c. It provides a specific focus

People often have many ideas about goals and methods of change; solution focused thinking helps to put these in an order which is practical and accessible.

"It gave a plan, a focus."

"The guidance and structure provided by the interviews ... gave me a very clear plan and framework which was understood and (almost) designed by the boys themselves."

"The scaling questions ... really gave a very practical and personal objective."

"Thinking about things before you do it."

"It helped focus on his individual needs rather than a more general approach."

d. The interaction pattern between people changes

In solution focused thinking the focus on exceptions, strengths, and so on, does seem to encourage the emergence of new ways of talking and relating between people.

> "I became curious ... I felt I knew what to ask ... I needed him as much as he needed me."

> "We were engaged in a joint venture ... it felt like we made a journey together."

> "We had to build up a working relationship of trust ... spend the time early on to talk with each other."

> "Their active involvement and the value placed upon their ideas and opinions increased the chances of success considerably."

> "It gave Elaine and I a way of talking about spelling which was positive."

> "Find a shared passion."

> "I understand his needs better."

> "I changed friends ... I used to boss my friends about ... to read for me."

e. It suggests the possibility of experimenting

Sometimes people become locked into one way of doing things: solution focused thinking encourages people to experiment and assess situations in a non judgmental dialogue with others.

> "I found the most useful thing (was) ... trying out different approaches."

> "It was particularly useful to come to an understanding that there are different ways that people can learn how to spell. It was then useful to try out the different methods systematically."

Some theoretical issues

Psychological models

Different solution focused therapists tend to draw on diverse background models in psychology. Some state that their thinking is influenced by systemic ideas, for example, the writings of Furman and

Ahola (1992). Other writers have stated that they prefer the term "interactional". Cade and O'Hanlon (1993) comment, "We no longer use the systemic paradigm as our main model."

Hence it would seem that the practice of solution focused work can draw on more than one model of social and individual psychology. In the writings of solution focused workers, however, the following themes are frequently found:

a) an emphasis on meaning, language, perception, beliefs, ideas, personal constructs (Kelly, 1955, who is mentioned particularly by Cade and O'Hanlon 1993).

b) an interest in the concepts of interaction and patterns which emerge in social situations. That is, how people do things, use language, act with each other, the sequence of events and the ideas concerning these things.

We would argue that a useful source of ideas for solution focused thinking might be those psychologies which emphasise the above themes, such as Harré(1979), Harré and Secord(1972), or those theories which look at how language is used in social situations (Potter and Wetherell, 1987).

In practical situations, however, the essential sources of concepts and language are, of course, the persons involved.

The problem-solving model

Some psychologists and others reading this book may have considered whether the solution focused model seems to contradict certain ideas of systematic problem-solving, particularly the versions based on behavioural psychology (see Cameron in Scherer et al, eds., 1990). The latter model suggests, among other things, a listing and prioritising of problems and an extensive collection of information on the chosen problem. However, in several chapters we have suggested minimal data collection and other steps which certainly do not conform to this model. We are not sure if the solution focused approach is a rejection of the problem-solving model or simply an alternative method. In some views, solution focused work is essentially a conversation whose parts cannot be analysed into distinct phases of assessment and intervention. However, in those contexts where an official report is required Durrant has developed various creative methods of assessment which focus on strengths instead of high-lighting failings and faults (Durrant, 1993, chapter three). Without entering into a detailed theoretical debate, we do believe that using solution focused thinking raises questions in at least the following areas:

- How much assessment of the problem is really needed?
- Are there clear stages or sequences between assessment and intervention?
- What are the most useful or necessary areas to focus on?
- What is the nature of the link between intervention and assessment?
- What are the social and psychological effects of investigating problems, particularly on self-esteem and hope?.

Some educational psychologists have questioned the applicability of the problem-solving model. For example, Halliwell and Williams (1990) offer as an alternative a model which focuses on the process of reaching decisions about which solutions to pursue in the context of potentially difficult meetings. Perhaps future work will look at when one model is more suitable than another.

Does the Solution Focused approach work?
Is there any scientific proof of the effectiveness of solution focused therapy? Some research has been carried out by de Shazer and his team (1991) and their results seem comparable to other therapeutic effectiveness research (see Smith et al, 1980, for a major review). This comparative research suggests, given certain conditions and qualifications, that all therapies are more or less equivalent in outcome. If this is so, should we not then choose therapies which are simple, short term, and respectful of the person?

We have stated often how struck we have been by the practical nature of this approach. We can only speculate why this is so, but would suggest the following as relevant:

- de Shazer and his team made a direct observational study of the actual interactions between clients and therapists, and hence grounded their theory in this, as opposed to relying on the therapist's memory of what happened. Furthermore, the team has become very interested in the language used in sessions, the 'conversation' (de Shazer, 1991). All this has facilitated a clear and accessible description of the therapeutic process which does not rely on just abstract constructs.

- They actively tried to find the simplest method that 'worked' and did not rely on theories of pathology (for example, what the origin and cause of depression might be), personality or development. Furthermore, they made these methods explicit.

Some readers may have asked the question: do clients feel listened to if there is such an emphasis on solutions and so forth? Llewelyn (1988) carried out research examining how clients and therapists perceived their experience of sessions and then correlated this with outcome. This research did not examine solution focused work, but psychodynamic and behavioural approaches. The three elements most valued by clients were solutions to problems, reassurance and contact. The results suggested that clients 'are most interested in gaining a solution to their problems and feeling better, whereas therapists are more concerned with the aetiology of the problem and its transformation through insight'. The research also suggested that the greater the difference of perception between therapist and client, then the poorer the outcome.

Final thoughts

What has been presented in this book is a detailed discussion about solution focused thinking and its application to our work in schools. The intention has not been to present it as a panacea, but we have certainly been encouraged and inspired by it. Because of its flexibility, the possibilities for development seem wide-ranging and we heartily recommend it as a useful addition to the repertoire of those working with young people and teachers in schools.

Bibliography

Recommended Reading

de Shazer, S. (1985) **Keys to Solution in Brief Therapy.** New York: Norton.

de Shazer, S. (1988) **Clues: Investigating Solutions in Brief Therapy.** New York: Norton.

Furman, B. and Ahola, T. (1992) **Solution Talk: Hosting Therapeutic Conversations.** New York: Norton.

George, E. Iveson, C. and Ratner, H. (1990) **Problem to Solution.** BT Press.

O'Hanlon, W. and Weiner-Davis, M. (1989) **In Search of Solutions.** New York: Norton.

White, M. and Epston, D. (1990) **Narrative Means to Therapeutic Ends.** New York: Norton.

References

Aponte, H. J. (1976) 'The family-school interview: an ecostructural approach', *Family Process 15*, 303-13.

Brewin, C. (1988) **Cognitive Foundations of Clinical Psychology.** New York: Lawrence Erlbaum Association.

Berg, I. K. (1991) **Family Preservation - A Brief Therapy Workbook.** BT Press.

Brown, A.L. and Deloache, J.S. (1983) **Metacognitive Skills**, in: Donaldson, M. (ed) *Early Childhood Development and Education.* Oxford Blackwells.

Bryant, P. and Bradley, L. (1985) **Children's Reading Problems.** Blackwell.

Burden, R. (1978) 'Schools' System Analysis: a project-centred approach', in Gillham, B.(Ed)(1978) *Reconstructing Educational Psychology.* Croom Helm.

Butkowsky, I.S. and Williams, D.M. (1980) **Cognitive-Motivational char-acteristics of children varying in reading ability; evidence of learned**

helplessness in poor readers. *Journal of Educational Psychology*, *72*, *3*, (pp 408-22).

Cade, B and O'Hanlon, W.H. (1993) **A Brief Guide to Brief Therapy.** London: Norton.

Cameron, R. J. and Stratford, R. J. (1987) **'Educational Psychology: a problem centred approach to service delivery'**, *Educational Psychology in Practice*, *2 (4)* 10-21.

Campbell, D., Draper, R. and Huffington, C. (1989) **A Systemic Approach to Consultation.** Draper Campbell: London.

Caplan, G. (1970) **The Theory and Practice of Mental Health Consultation.** London: Tavistock Publications.

Checkland, P.B. (1981) **Systems Thinking, Systems Practice.** London: Wiley.

Cohen, L. and Manion, L. (1985) **Research Methods in Education** (2nd Edition). Croom Helm.

Deci, E.L. and Ryan, R.M. (1985) **Intrinsic Motivation and Self Determination in Human Behaviour.** Plenum.

de Shazer, S. (1984) **'The Death of Resistance'**, *Family Process*, *23*, 70-83.

de Shazer, S. (1985) **Keys to Solution in Brief Therapy.** New York: Norton.

de Shazer, S. (1988) **Clues: Investigating Solutions in Brief Therapy.** New York: Norton.

de Shazer, S. (1991) **Putting Difference to Work.** New York: Norton.

de Shazer, S. (1994) **Words Were Originally Magic.** New York: Norton.

de Shazer, S. and Berg, I.K. (1991) **'Reluctant Clients'.** Conference organised by the Brief Therapy Practice. London.

Dolan, Y. (1991) **Resolving Sexual Abuse: Solution Focused Therapy and Eriksonian Hypnosis for Adult Survivors.** Norton.

Dowling, E. and Osborne, E. (eds), (1985) **The Family and the School.** London: Routledge & Kegan Paul.

Durrant, M. (1993) **Residential Treatment: A cooperative, competency based approach to therapy and progress design.** Norton.

Durrant, M. (1993) **Creative Strategies for School Problems.** Eastwood Family Therapy Centre.

Epston, D. (1989) **Collected Papers.** Dulwich Centre Publications.

Epston, D. and White, M. (1992) **Experience, Contradictions, Narrative and Imagination.** Dulwich Centre Publications.

Fox, M. and Sigston, A. (1992) **Connecting Organisational Psychology, Schools and Educational Psychologists,** in Wolfendale, S. (Ed, et al) (1992) *The Profession and Practice of Educational Psychology.* Cassell.

Frank, J.D. (1986) **Psychotherapy - the transformation of meanings: discussion paper.** *Journal of the Royal Society of Medicine, Vol 79,* June 1986.

Frederickson, N. (1991) (Ed) **Soft Systems Methodology: Applications in E.P. Practice.** U.C.L.

Furman, B. and Ahola, T. (1988) 'The return of the question why: the advantages of exploring pre-existing explanations'. *Family Process, 27(4)* (pp 395-409)

Furman, B. and Ahola, T. (1992) **Solution Talk: Hosting Therapeutic Conversations.** New York: Norton.

Gentile, L.M. and McMillan, M.M. (1987) **Stress and Reading Difficulties: Research, Assessment and Intervention. Newark, D.E:** International Reading Association.

George, E. Iveson, C. and Ratner, H. (1990) **Problem to Solution.** BT Press.

Geordiades, N. and Phillimore, L. (1975) 'The myth of the hero innovator and alternative strategies for organisational change', in Kiernan, C.C. and Woodford, F.P., *Behaviour modification with the severely retarded.* Amsterdam: IRMMH Study Group Associated Scientific Papers.

Gillham, B. **Reconstructing Educational Psychology.** London: Croom Helm.

Gurney, P. (1990) 'Using behavioural contracts in the classroom', in Scherer, M., Gersch, I. and Fry, L.: *Meeting Disruptive Behaviour.* Routledge.

Haley, J. (1963) **Strategies of Psychotherapy.** New York: Grune and Stratton.

Haley, J. (1973) **Uncommon Therapy: The psychiatric techniques of Milton H. Erickson M.D.** New York: Norton.

Haley, J. (1973) **Uncommon Therapy.** New York: Norton.

Halliwall, M. D. and Williams, T. L. (1992) 'Towards more effective decision making in assessment: Pathway-meeting the needs of all pupil', in Cline, T. (eds) *Assessment of Special Educational Needs*. London: Routledge.

Harre, R. (1979) **Social Being**. Blackwell.

Harre, R. and Secord, P.F. (1972) **The Explanation of Social Behaviour**. Blackwell.

Jones, N. and Frederickson, N. (Eds) (1990) **Refocusing Educational Psychology**. London: The Falmer Press.

Kelley, G. (1955) **The Psychology of Personal Constructs**. New York: W.W. Norton.

Kohl, H. (1973) **Reading, How To**. Dutton.

Kral, R. (1978) **Strategies that Work: Techniques for Solution in the Schools**. Milwaukee: BFTC.

Lawrence, D. (1973) **Improving Reading through Counselling**. London: Ward Lock.

Lawrence, D. (1985) 'Improving self esteem and reading', Educational Research, 27, 3, (pp194-200).

Lethem, J. (1994) **Moved to tears, moved to action**. London: BT Press.

Lipchick, E. (1987) **Interviewing**. Rockville: Aspen.

Lipchick, E. and de Shazer, S. (1986) 'The purposeful interview', *Journal of Strategic and Systemic Therapies*. 5 (1), 88-99.

Llewelyn, S.P. (1988) **Psychological therapy as viewed by clients and therapists**. *British Journal of Clinical Psychology*, Vol 27, Part 3.

Locke, E., Shaw, K., Saari, L., and Latham, G. (1981) 'Goal setting and Task performance': 1969 - 1980, *Psychological Bulletin*, 90, (pp 125-152).

Measor, L. and Woods, P. (1984) **Changing Schools**. Milton Keynes: Open University Press.

Molnar, A. and Linquist, B. (19889) **Changing Problem Behaviour in School**. New York: Jossey-Bass.

O'Hanlon, W. (1987) **Taproots**. New York: Norton.

O'Hanlon, W. and Weiner-Davis, M. (1989) **In Search of Solutions**. New York: Norton.

Porter, J. and Rourke, B.P. (1985) 'Socio-emotional functioning of learning disabled children: a subtypal analysis of personality patterns'. In: Rourke, B.P. (Ed) *Neuropsychology of Learning Disabilities: Essentials of Subtype Analysis.* New York: Guildford Press.

Potter, J. and Wetherell, M. (1987) **Discourse and Social Psychology: Beyond Attitudes and Behaviour.** Sage Publications.

Rhodes, J. (1987) **Action Research with a Difficult Class** (Unpublished dissertation, Institute of Education, London University).

Rhodes, J. (1993) 'The use of solution focused brief therapy in schools', *Educational Psychology in Practice Vol 9, No 1* (pp 27 - 34).

Rossi, E.L. (Ed) (1980) **The Collected Papers of Milton H. Erickson, M.D.** (4 volumes). New York: Irvington.

Rutter, M., Maughan, B., Mortimore, P. and Ouston, J. (1979) **Fifteen Thousand Hours.** London: Open Books.

Schmuck, R.A., and Schmuck, P.A. (1971) **Group Processes in the Classroom.** Dubaque, Ia.: W.C. Brown.

Smith, F. (1971) **Understanding Reading.** New York: Holt, Rinehart and Winston.

Smith, M. L., Glass, G. V. and Miller, T. I. (1980) **The Benefits of Psychotherapy.** Baltimore: Johns Hopkins.

Solity, J. and Bull, S. (1987) **Special Needs: Bridging the Curriculum Gap.** O.U. Press.

Tharp, R.G. and Wetzel, R.J. (1969) **Behaviour Modification in the Natural Environment.** Academic Press.

Tomm, K. (1987) **Interventive Interviewing: Part I. Strategising as a fourth guide for the therapist.** *Family Processes, 26:* 3-13.

Topping, K. (1988) **Peer Tutoring Handbook: Promoting Co-operative Learning.** London: Croom Helm.

Watzlawick, P., Weakland, J., and Fisch, R. (1974) **Change: Principles of Problem Formations and Problem Resolution.** New York: Norton.

Weakland. J. H., Fisch, R., Watzlawick, P. and Bodin, A. A. (1974) '**Brief therapy: focused problem resolution**', *Family Process. 13,* 141-168.

Weiner-Davis, M., de Shazer, S., and Gingerich, W. J., (1987) '**Using pretreatment change to construct a therapeutic solution: a note**'. *Journal of Martial and Family Therapy, 13* (pp) 359-363.

White, M. (1989) **Selected Papers.** Dulwich Centre Publications.

White, M. and Epston, D. (1990) **Narrative Means to Therapeutic Ends.** New York: Norton.

Wright, J. and Cashdan, A. (1991) **Training Metacognitive Skills in Backward Readers: A Pilot Study,** *Educational Psychology in Practice Vol 7, No 3.* (pp 153-162).

Wolfendale,S., Bryans, T., Fox,M., Labram, A. and Sigston, A. (1992) **The Profession and Practice of Educational Psychology.** Cassell.

Wolfgang, C. and Glickman, C. (1986) **Solving Discipline Problems: Strategies for classroom Teachers.** Boston: Allyn and Bacon.